# MY OTHER EX

*Women's True Stories of Leaving and
Losing Friends*

JESSICA SMOCK AND STEPHANIE
SPRENGER

*HerStories Project Press*

MY OTHER EX: WOMEN'S TRUE STORIES OF LOSING AND LEAVING FRIENDS

Copyright © 2014 by HerStories Project, LLC

ISBN: 978-0-692-27258-9

Printed in the United States of America

Cover Photo by KC Photography, Cincinatti, Ohio

*To Adrian and Gavin – JAS*

*For Shannon— I'm so glad we found our way
back together. – SCS*

# CONTENTS

# FOREWORD

---

NICOLE KNEPPER

"And yet women—good women—frightened me because they eventually wanted your soul, and what was left of mine, I wanted to keep."—Charles Bukowski

Charles Bukowski's 1978 novel, *Women*, is often chided as an obscene, misogynistic, drunken rant. Maybe it is, but damn if his raw tirades and ferocity against women don't provide some of the clearest illustrations of how women require such an overwhelming intensity in their relationships with each other. Albeit crudely and crassly, Chuck nailed it.

Most women crave visceral connections and mutual comprehension, and we achieve it on the regular, because we are innately capable of doing so; that's just how we're built. And that, my friends, is essentially why women really only find this type of connection in relationships with other women. It's also why the loss of these relationships is so damn profound and painful, why the stories in this book are so mother*cking poignant.

Women have some serious soul-sucking tendencies. In many of our relationships, we *do* demand and passionately pursue nothing less than unlimited access to the depths of another's soul. I guess Aristotle described it in a more palatable and polite way when he said that friendship is a single soul dwelling in two bodies. I prefer Chuck's salacious histrionics, but Ari has a good point. What is a friendship without the merging of souls? (What? I'm sweary and blunt, but I'm not heartless.)

And this soul connection is tricky! Two bodies, like darkness and light, are by nature distinct. Chew on that for just a second, because it's the true taste of friendship—two separate bodies, yet a necessary and complementary connectedness that is often bittersweet. So is the tone of this collection of deeply personal stories about leaving and losing friends.

I was stupidly excited to be asked to write the foreword for this book and eagerly awaited a sample of some of the melancholy and emotional essays that would be included. I am attracted to the dark like a moth to a flame. (I'm a weirdo, I know.) I was anticipating painful and candid revelations, and I was delighted to see that each author generously offered an unabashed view into the dark side of her heart. It made me feel like less of a freak. That's the point of the collection, too! Why stew alone in guilt and shame over the times you were selfish, envious, angry, or indifferent toward a friend when you can stew among others?

I'm happy to tell you that this book is going to be a bittersweet read. You will learn stuff, and I am a huge fan of people learning, even if that process is somewhat painful. Did Aristotle also say, "No pain, no gain."? I digress. The confessions might be graphic and ugly, because the heartache and the agony in these essays is authentic. This isn't an easy, breezy beach read. You will hurt for the women telling their stories, feel the intensity of their struggles, re-grieve your own losses and, within these words about loss, quite possibly come to the realization that an impending one might be coming your way.

Women are frustratingly and magnificently wired for intimacy. As we experience social role changes that increase our responsibilities, we instinctively seek out and rely on female relationships to help us define these ever-changing roles. In the process, we learn how to spot our soul sisters. It's not uncommon to grow in and out of situational friendships over time, but some of the relationships we build feel Aristotle-quote-worthy.

It's these soul-connecting friendships that we hope will survive the inevitable physical and emotional separations that happen over time. When they don't, whether the loss is a slow burnout or a blowout that shatters the seemingly unbreakable bond so completely it can never be repaired, it's a sort of death, and it's just the worst, because it's so damn confusing and incomplete.

The loss of a friend who continues to live and breathe is as painful, if not more so, than saying a physical goodbye to a lifeless body ravaged by disease or a tragic accident. How do you say goodbye when you still have to mutter the occasional hello? How do you grieve a heart that beats just out of your reach? How do resist slashing a bitch's tires? Oh, I'm just kidding.

Sort of.

The authors of the essays in *My Other Ex* attempt to answer these questions, by taking you with them on their journeys of grief and growth. Grieving the loss of a friendship is, unfortunately, as unpredictable and demanding a process as growing one. Each stage of the breakup requires infinite patience and rapt attention to the inevitable pain as it evolves and infiltrates every fiber of your being. Forever.

If grief were a gender, it would certainly be a woman, because the only thing besides a woman that seeks to permanently invade the depths of your soul is the infinite emotion of grief. I'm sure someone is offended by what I just said about women being as demanding as grief, but I care not, because the anger only validates its beautiful and terrible truth.

Simply put—losing a beloved soul sister sucks. Not having to do it alone sucks less. That's why I'm glad you found *My Other Ex*. I am supremely confident that as you read the words of wisdom here, you *will* find a comfort, connectedness and heart-healing that only the transformative power of shared experience can provide.

*Nicole Knepper is a Licensed Clinical Professional Counselor with two advanced degrees (psychology and gerontology) whose blog,* Moms Who Drink And Swear™, *became the basis for her first book,* Moms Who Drink and Swear: True Tales of Loving My Kids While Losing My Mind. *Nikki, sometimes referred to as the Queen of Cussin', creates, edits, and curates content for her million fans strong Facebook page,* Moms Who Drink And Swear™ *and for her Moms Who Drink And Swear™ blogs. She devotes significant time and space on her massive social media platform to raise awareness and funds for charitable organizations and regularly hosts fundraising events.*

# INTRODUCTION

_____

JESSICA SMOCK

"I grieved it hard. I talked to only a few close friends, in spite of being a real talker, because I felt such shame about it."

"I was broken. This was my best friend from the fifth grade up into young adulthood. I don't know if I ever have truly moved on. I still miss her."

"I felt like I'd lost a part of myself. I had a hollow feeling inside all the time. I'd pick up the phone to call her (we used to chat for hours a day) and remember I couldn't call her, and I'd cry."

"I went into a deep depression that lasted for four years, during which I couldn't make any other friends."

"I felt humiliated and confused. Even now when I think about it, I can still feel how rejected and small I felt when it happened."

That last quote was mine. The rest are from a few of the dozens of women that took the time to respond to our survey about friendship loss, others who wrote to us, or those that we spoke to in person or online when researching this book. Women who still carried around the hurt of failed or lost friendships.

While the details of the individual stories vary—dissolutions due to betrayals and boyfriends, others falling apart under the stress of competition and envy, and many more friendships fading away with age and life transitions—the feelings that women shared with us about their breakups were surprisingly similar.

During the first days and weeks following the loss of a friendship, when the fact of it is so raw and sharp, we've learned from women that it's typical to feel most alone, to feel embarrassed, depressed, shocked, and obsessed with why and how it happened. You often feel heartbroken, as if you've lost a great love. And you have. Not a romantic partner but a trusted holder of your secrets and truths.

Sometimes that pain never truly goes away. It's a dull ache that can return when a familiar song is heard, a movie line is repeated, a Facebook status appears, or an old picture falls out of an album.

It surprised me at first to learn that so many of the women who answered our survey chose to tell us about friendships that ended long ago. In fact, the most frequent time period of friendship loss identified by women in our survey was childhood and adolescence. Including college, these essays make up nearly half of the collection.

The friendship that I'm describing in my own quote above ended during my first year of high school, and the details come back to me like the events happened yesterday.

I grew up in a rural town in the Adirondacks of upstate New York. You knew everyone, and everyone's family, and everyone knew you. It was easy to be pigeon-holed as a small child. Early character traits were seized upon as permanent identifiers. You were "a baseball kid" or the "bad boy" or "the funny girl" or "one of the smart kids." That was who you were. End of story. Forever.

I was a smart girl, maybe even a nerd. I was not in the popular crowd, and wasn't entirely sure that I wanted to be, but I was still fascinated by them, the girls, especially in junior high. How their hair was always carefully blown out high and hair-sprayed, how they found the perfect shade of scrunchy sock to match every shirt, how their skin never seemed to show pimples. I had many friends that I adored, but I knew none of us was popular. We were a collection of smart, awkward good girls. Alone in my room, reading about the adventures of the more glamorous and fun-loving Jessica of Sweet Valley High, I wondered if I had it in me to be a popular girl too.

I also had a secret crush. My crush was on Brandon, one of the most popular guys in my grade. Serendipitously, I sat next to him in two classes, our last names alphabetically close, and I let him copy my history quizzes, gave him homework answers, and smiled and giggled shyly as he whispered to me during class. But I knew Brandon was way out of my league. Because I wasn't a cool kid.

By the time a new girl, Diane, moved to town, I had begun to get restless. I secretly wished that my friends could try a little harder to fit in with the popular kids, and I became resentful. Diane was from out of state, a rarity in our parts, and she immediately looked out of place. Her hair was thick and straight—no perm, no layers—and she wore no makeup. She dressed in L.L. Bean and J. Crew, a style that I now could easily identify as "preppy," but was a uniform entirely out of place in our working class, rural town.

But despite her differences, I instinctively recognized that she would, at some point, be popular. She was funny and outgoing, and most importantly for a girl she was pretty. I wasn't an outgoing kid, but I pushed myself to be friendly with Diane. Soon we were walking to class together, and she had invited me over to her house for a sleepover. She ate with my friends at lunch. Weeks later she invited me to go on a day trip with her whole family to a new city.

As our friendship grew closer over the semester, the popular girls were making their own advances. Diane was invited to dances with them, to the mall, to their own sleepovers. Soon she was too busy for me, and she no longer looked for me and my friends in the cafeteria. She had her own table with the popular kids. As the months passed, she wouldn't speak to me for days or wouldn't look up when I entered the classroom.

Then one spring day I journeyed to the nearest mall with my mom. It was a quick trip, and we had gone our separate ways once we got there. I normally didn't walk around the mall alone, without a friend, but that day I didn't mind. By that point, I already knew that I would be going away to boarding school in the fall, away from our town, and on to much more exciting possibilities.

Coming in the opposite direction toward the food court, I saw Diane walking hand in hand with Brandon, my crush. I had imagined that he could still fall in love with me by the end of the school year, and we'd exchange love letters while I was at boarding school. Diane walked right past me and said nothing. By this time, her hair had been permed and hair-sprayed like all the other popular girls, and she wore a thick armor of makeup. When she passed me, she gave no nod of acknowledgement, not even a slight smile. Brandon ignored me too. I felt worthless, invisible. There was no question: Diane didn't consider me to be a friend. No matter how smart I was perceived to be by my classmates, or how welcoming I had been to her, no matter how far away I would go to school, I still wasn't worthy of her friendship. I still wasn't a cool kid. I had never felt rejection that stung like that before. I was wounded and humiliated, and I shrank back from everyone, even my true friends, during those last months before boarding school.

Even as I write this, I know my story isn't particularly compelling or unusual. After reading hundreds of friendship breakup stories, ones with far more provocative and expertly told plots, I could have guessed the resolution before the exposition was finished. Two girls are friends. One of the friends begins to become more popular than the other. The other girl abandons the first girl silently and cruelly. The first girl is broken-hearted, and the other one moves on blindly. How many times and in how many ways has that tale of connection, hope, trust, and loss been told?

We started this book looking for answers. We wanted to know why these stories resonated so deeply with women, years and decades later, revealing wounds deeper than the scars left from romantic relationships. We wanted to know why women's friendships begin and end so differently than men's. We wanted to know why women seemed to feel more guilt, more shame, more trauma, and more remorse about the ends of friendships than the loss of romantic partners.

I wish I could report that we found definitive answers to these questions. But there are no startling conclusions. We can describe patterns and speculation, but in many ways we still feel just as confused and in awe of the power of friendship to support and comfort, as well as hurt and destroy, as we did when we started the project.

As experts in the field of friendship have described in many books and articles, there is a dark side to female friendship. Yes, there is unparalleled closeness, connection, support, and love, but there are also millions of women who carry around deep scars from painful relationships. Kelly Valen is a journalist whose own story of friendship heartache, published the *New York Times*, went viral and became the basis of a research study and, later, book called *The Twisted Sisterhood: Unraveling the Dark Legacy of Female Friendship*s. She heard hundreds of women's stories through her own survey and reporting. Based on her research, she wrote:

> We're not talking about just a few intimacy-challenged sisters with mean-girl episodes on the brain. I'm seeing widespread, corrosive brand of ambivalence among all types of women and a whole lot of hidden, unresolved anxiety, frustration, annoyance, and residual hurt that hasn't found a voice.

What Valen found—and what Stephanie and I discovered as well—is that these patterns and this hurt can start very early in a girl's life. It can begin on the playgrounds and in elementary school classrooms. Even today, young girls are still socialized—and rewarded by parents, teachers, and other adults—to be "good girls." While boys stereotypically handle conflict with physical and verbal aggression or more direct forms of confrontation, girls know that nice girls should never appear outwardly mean. They quickly learn that the socially acceptable way to channel their anger and feelings is to take them underground. They become masters at the subtle arts of exclusion, gossip, withholding friendship strategically, and other forms of manipulation to get their way with uncooperative peers and friends.

Girls become adept at what researchers call *indirect* or *relational aggression*. Rachel Simmons' research in the bestselling book *Odd Girl Out: The Hidden Culture of Aggression in Girls*, as well as Cheryl Dellasega's study of adult women in *Mean Girls Grown Up*, demonstrate that these strategies of using subtle emotional devastation to manage conflict can last a lifetime. Females learn to use relationships themselves as weapons—rather than fists, direct demands, and screaming. Their tools are the ability to undermine, manipulate, betray, and ignore. The devastation wrought can appear unintentional and difficult to describe or identify, sometimes masked by the careful image of the polite good girl.

When I read through the research on conflict in female friendships, so much of it rang true to my experience, in ways that I never thought about or acknowledged. There is so much good, so much power, so much love, in female friendships. But there is also a dark side of pain and loss. And surrounding that dark side, there is often silence. Women feel that there is no language to talk about their feelings. There is shame, the haunting feeling that the loss of a friendship is a reflection of our own worth or capacity to be loved.

This book, we hope, is a step toward breaking that silence. We as women need to recognize the scars of lost friendships and make it okay to talk about them. And we must also teach our daughters how to manage conflict and emotion without resorting to these forms of indirect aggression that cause deep pain with no visible wounds.

The life cycle is long, and many friendships will not last. Yet the end of something once powerful and important will bring sadness and grief, feelings that deserve to be acknowledged.

In the first section of this collection—"When We're Young"—you'll read about friendships begun and lost during childhood, adolescence, and the earliest years of adulthood. You'll read about friends who break young girls' hearts and others whose hearts have been broken.

The second section—"When We're Grown Up"—contains stories of friendships that strain and struggle in part because of the challenges of adulthood: work, marriage, infidelity, illness. The third section—"Motherhood"—includes pieces that explore the effects of children—their presence or absence—on a friendship. In "Reconciliations," the next section, you'll read about relationships that fall apart and then begin again, sometimes tentative and fractured, sometimes as if no rupture ever happened.

The last part of the book—"Reflections"—begins with a powerful introduction by my co-editor, Stephanie, which includes her own story of a friendship break. The rest of the essays in this section are not so much individual stories but deep (and often critical) examinations of friendship breakups and loss in these writers' lives.

We are thankful to the brave women who shared their stories about complicated relationships, relationships that were forged not through blood or romance but through companionship and emotional connection. Their stories haunted them, they haunted us, and we know that they will move you too.

# WHEN WE'RE YOUNG

# A LETTER TO A

VICTORIA FEDDEN

Dear A,

I lost your mother's pear cake recipe. It happened during one of the five times I moved since I got the letter from you asking me never to call or write again. When I discovered that the recipe was gone, I panicked. I searched everywhere for it or for recipes that were similar. I found nothing close and then I tried to think of mutual friends I could enlist to get the recipe from you, pretending they wanted it for themselves. You'd see through that though, because you knew how much I loved the pear cake. You would remember the time you promised to make it for me once the blizzard passed and the electricity came back on. I would hate for you to know I lost the recipe and I hate to think of you saying that of course I lost the recipe, how it was just like me to lose the recipe because I was always careless like that, even with the things I loved most. But I'm not like that now and it's important you know that. A lot about me has changed.

Since we last spoke, most importantly, I learned to

write. I learned about not using vague descriptives, to find the most unexpected metaphors and the most concrete nouns. Once a teacher told me that my writing has to make me cry and that I have to be brave and write about my hurt and stop just trying to make people laugh. She said I try to be funny so that people will love me.

That's what we all want ultimately—for everyone to love us, and I have written a lot about the people who do love me, but not so much about the people, like you, who don't. I feel like I might cry if I wrote about you. I'm petrified of crying, or of people knowing that I cry or of people seeing me as anything other than light-hearted. I've based a whole new life on being the happy girl who doesn't cry. And then I sob when I see a TV show about a polar bear swimming for miles looking for an ice floe to rest upon, finding nothing but saltwater and drowning from exhaustion.

At some point I told myself that the one thing I would never write about was us, because if I did, you would be upset. You would say I was being an exhibitionist, that I told the story wrong, that I painted myself more favorably, that I humiliated you. Perhaps you'd be right. I know I couldn't write it without lying by omission, and so I won't write our story at all. This is not our story. I'm only writing here about how much I miss you, how I regret what happened and how I've changed.

My own stupidity, insecurity, and lack of character led to the end of our friendship. We had been friends for over a decade when it happened. We met when we were 11 and last spoke when we were 24. You ended it with the letter, which I always suspected your therapist instructed you to write. I imagined the scene where you spent an entire appointment complaining about my constant phone calls, my stinging comments whenever something good happened to you that did not also happen to me, how I behaved inappropriately around others because I simply didn't know better. You might throw in how you had grown and I hadn't. Ivy-League educated and well-traveled, you were now beginning a career while I, with my GED, had no résumé, no degrees, and couldn't keep up with an intellectual conversation. The therapist probably talked about how people grow apart and how childhood friendships often must end in adulthood and how you had to cut me off.

A letter would be the best way. End it swiftly and utterly, the therapist would say. She would explain to you that I needed consequences for my behavior and that if you continued your friendship with me I would continue to torment you, to sap your energy, becoming more and more toxic and difficult to purge from your life. Maybe it didn't happen that way at all, but I still have the letter you sent.

When I'm not regretful about our friendship, I am hopeful. As teenagers we fought all the time. I probably started every argument we ever had, in all fairness. We would fight and then stop speaking sometimes for weeks or months at a time. My hopeful, idealistic self convinces me that this is just another one of those incidents, one that has lasted ten years, but still a temporary hiatus in what will be a lifelong friendship, what *has* to be a lifelong friendship, because no one has ever loved a friend like we loved each other. And I think one day we will laugh about this and then we'll cry because we wasted ten years and missed milestones and then we'll laugh again because we used to laugh all the time. When I'm hopeful I feel like I'm still 15.

I wish that I could say: A, I am sorry, but forgive me because I was young and insecure and every horrible moment I created was based on my feelings of worthlessness because I believed I was unlovable and my want was like a tantrum. What I wanted was to be like you. I felt the world cheated me out of the opportunities you had and that I too should sail the Virgin Islands, study in Brighton and work in publishing, instead of toiling in restaurant kitchens that made me reek of fried fish and garlic.

I want you to know that now I am your equal, that I also have accomplishments and because I've been able to haul myself up out of my misery and worthlessness I'm not so insecure anymore. I'm just as educated as you. I bought myself a plane ticket and claimed Paris as my own. I have a husband who loves me a thousand more times than I deserve, and because of this I've created myself as this funny, charming, silly girl, full of self-deprecation and self-help. I throw fabulous dinner parties, though I've often wished I could bake and serve the pear cake for my guests. I belong to a book club and there are many, many people who think I'm fun and interesting. I do all the same things you do, like shop at IKEA, pay too much for flavored sea salts to make recipes I read about in *Saveur*. I read *The New York Times*. I'd also like to throw in that I'm a published writer. I'd like you to know that, but that would be bragging, wouldn't it, and would that mean that maybe I haven't changed so much at all?

I'm still competitive, just not as often and not in such a raw, despairing way. I don't need to act out my feelings of not-good-enough in that way anymore. I've given that up. I confess that I read your husband's blog. Paranoid, I don't read it too often because I don't want him or you to see that I'm reading it. Mostly I just wait for him to post pictures of you, which he rarely does, and then I look at them for a long, long time. But not too long, because you might know. But then, not long enough. I try to determine if you're happy. I want you to be happy. I want to lie about the fact that I examined one of the pictures to determine if I was still thinner than you. I concluded that we are the exact same size, and then I was miserable that I compared myself to you again after a decade of missing you, making wishes about you.

Comparing is my worst habit. I compared myself to you. That was my tragic flaw, or one of my tragic flaws in all of this. White trash, uneducated, unsophisticated and ignorant, I never measured up. I still compare. I have compared every single female friend I've made since you, to you. None of them has come close.

One of the wishes I make is that I would run into you somewhere by chance. I play this one out a few different ways. Most scenarios have you being happy to see me. We hug. There are tears and apologies and we must have tea and tea becomes dinner. The restaurant closes and we are still there. We leave intertwined. We used to walk that way all the time singing, so we begin to sing again, remembering the words to "Just Like Heaven." We go home and there is the pear cake with slivered almonds and whipped cream. You copy down the recipe for me again and tease me about losing it. We talk and at some point in the night I am brushing your hair which crackles with static. There are many reasons why this could never happen and they are all my fault and they are a part of the story that I would not get right.

I wish for the Hollywood ending because in every romantic comedy there is a time when the characters are separated. The audience sees no hope for them to ever be together again. The situation is beyond repair and we fear all is lost, though really we know they are destined to be together; they *have* to be together. Our definition of love and good depends on their reunion and then after the grid-lock, a high speed chase ensues. One races toward the other. She is getting on the plane. They see each other at the gate. Don't leave. You see, it was all a misunderstanding and I love you. Yes, I love you and I have always loved you. I loved you from the moment I saw you and admit it, you love me too and we are meant to be together. Please come back to me. Please, I was an idiot and now I know I was wrong. I knew then. I knew the second I was away from you that all I ever wanted was to be your friend.

There are credits. Everyone in the theater moves towards the exit. The movie is over. You pull me out of my seat and we are swimming upstream through the bodies. We move in the opposite direction toward the stage, because the theater used to be a real theater with a stage and red velvet curtains, and then we are dancing on the stage. You lead. I am clumsy, but we are dancing across the blackness and the disappearing words. We laugh and dance. Do you remember when we did that?

Oh A, I am good enough now. I'm good. Look at how good I am.

Victoria

*Victoria Fedden lives with her family in Ft. Lauderdale, Florida and is the author of the memoirs* Amateur Night at the Bubblegum Kittikat *and* Sun Shower: Magic, Forgiveness and How I Learned to Bloom Where I Was Planted. *She received her MFA in Creative Writing from*

*Florida Atlantic University in 2009 and her work has appeared in* Real Simple, Chicken Soup for the Soul *and* The South Florida Sun Sentinel *plus several anthologies.*

# DELILAH

CHELSEA SCHOTT

*Duncan, Oklahoma*
  *1987*

I don't have a lot of friends. Actually, I don't have any. Before the morning bell rings and after Mama drops me off at the school corner, I spend twenty minutes aching in my solitude. Standing near the stair-cased entrance of Duncan Junior High, leaning against a brick wall under the unbearable weight of being self-conscious and shy. Hiding behind near-sighted lenses, a bad perm, and unfashionable off-brand sneakers.

*You'll make friends. Give it time. You're still new,* Mama says when I tell her of my isolation, my loneliest days.

In those solitary twenty minutes, when the morning sun is glinting through a tangle of live oak branches, I watch kids get dropped off, wander into groups with ease and confidence, being pulled as magnets, like droplets moving toward puddles. Joining into conversations, laughing about something that was said, coming together in that familiar, comfortable way friends do.

How I long for those moments. To draw myself up into a giggling huddle of girls my age, to hear them gush over some secret I revealed, for them to see me from a distance and wave with frantic arms, beckon me to come quick. Dying to tell me the news of some breakup, crush, or petty gossip. To roll their eyes over something we both dislike, to make surreptitious plans for meeting boys at the skating rink on a Friday night. To include my name on their list, to have my phone number memorized.

So I am desperate when I make friends with Delilah. She isn't my type. Black eye liner, heavy metal t-shirts and a pack of Marlboro lights in her backpack. The kind of girl Mama calls *bad news*. But I can't blame desperation. I love her. We dream of being artists, toil together over pre-algebra, spend hours talking about the latest movies, repeating our favorite lines in mocking voices and trying not to laugh under the hush of a rigid librarian.

On a day when I enter the cafeteria, ready to sit alone, my feet already on the course toward an empty table in the back corner, she links arms with me and brings me to her table. She introduces me as *friend*. In that moment, I know what it's like to be loved—to be shown off, to be bragged about, to have my heart knitted together with hers. Delilah talks about me in a way to her friends that makes me blush, look at the floor, unable to withhold my smile.

A few weeks later, when I say those words that bring us closer, she says them too, because we both feel it: *best friends*.

Delilah's crowd is rough. Children of bikers, drinkers, partiers. Most have parents in jail. Some have never met their own parents; I'm not that kind of kid. I can't even fake it. It's not my crowd.

They're the kind of kids who aren't kids long enough. Kids known by cops. The kind who know which clerks at the store will sell them booze, where the empty houses are, where the parties pop up on a Saturday night. How to find a clinic to get condoms and what exactly goes on behind a bowling alley. A common understanding moves between them, a group identity rooted in broken rules and broken homes.

Sure, Mama raises an eyebrow to Delilah, but says nothing. She must see my thrill in having a friend. And Delilah loves me when nobody else does. We spend entire weekends together, Delilah cooking for her elderly grandma, waiting for a collect call from jail—to hear her brother's voice—sneaking out her window, straddling a fat, black branch in an oak tree as she tries to get me to smoke some pot, coughing wildly against her fist. Dyeing my hair for the first time, her gloved fingers moving the inky black froth through my once blonde hair and laughing so hard when Mama rolls her eyes at the sight. Telling me how much she hates songs with her name in it and slugging me in the shoulder when I sing them anyway. Staying up so late our brains are numb and lame, laughing until we cry at something stupid one of us said. Or tried to say.

And here we are, sneaking off before the first tardy bell. If there is something dangerous, we long to know it. To peer into its black mysteries, to touch the edge of something forbidden. Her hand pulls forth a can of spray paint from her backpack, shaking it hard, hearing that tinny ball knock around inside the can and the hiss of paint against the stop sign as she blacks out the white letters. Running back to school just in time, my stomach full of clammy panic and my heart thumping fat and heavy in my chest, full of the wild fear that accompanies secrets and knowledge.

Delilah pushes the limits— it's what she does best. I can forgive her for coming to school high, for throwing away her virginity to a loser (even after I warned her with wide eyes and a wagging pointed finger). I can forgive her for showing up to the cafeteria every day without lunch money when her Daddy is laid off. I can forgive her shoplifting lip gloss right under my nose. I can forgive her for copying my history homework for the fourth time this week. Forgiveness comes easy for me, not for others.

When that rough crowd turns on her, shuns her in the cafeteria, passes her threatening notes in the hallway, promises a fist fight from a girl looking for trouble, I swear my protection. No one will ever touch Delilah, not on my watch. I have never been in a fight, but I am willing to try.

The next day, kids crowd the sidewalk before school, and the air holds a voltage I can feel. As the teachers dry up like a drought and disappear under the morning sun and kids chant *Fight! Fight! Fight!*, the school doors burst forth with the girls from that rough crowd.

As the biggest one holds her down, and punches her face until her nose breaks open with blood, the others dare me to move, to speak up, to do anything…

And I don't.

I can't speak up. I can't move. A panic surges through my chest. My allegiance evaporates under the glare of their hot eyes and clenched fists. And I watch as they beat the girl who loved me when no one else did, as she tries shielding her face, tries to stand on her feet.

I stand on that sidewalk, my face wet with hot tears under the morning sun, knowing I am failing her.

Standing there impotent, shaming myself, head shaking in cowardice, struggling under the unbearable weight of failing my only friend, unable to love her back like she deserves.

Teachers appear and drag the girls away. Delilah gets caught up between the nurse and principal and I lose her. I walk through my school day numb and alone, find a seat in the back of the lunch room, feet shuffling toward empty space in humiliation as eyes follow me across the cafeteria.

That night, when my courage waxes again, I dial Delilah's number. Hold the receiver close to my chin, swallow hard, desperate to know she's okay, reckless in remorse. At her *Hello*, my voice shakes across the line:

*Delilah. I'm so sorry. Are you okay?*

*Yes, yes. I'm okay. Suspended for the rest of the week.*

*God, I'm just –*

*Chelsea. It's okay. You're not like them. You're not a fighter.*

*I should've done something.*

*You couldn't have. Chelsea, you're not like us.*

*But I am, my Mama is a fighter, and I know how—*

*Chelsea. You'll never be like this. It's okay. It's why I love you.*

My heart breaks at the truth she knows, at a truth I cannot admit. Whatever courage I've tried to manufacture has failed me. I nurse a guilt that is deeply veined in every tissue of my being, threaded throughout every fiber of my body.

At Delilah's words, I cry. I cry because I did nothing for her and know I could do nothing for myself. Her voice echoes through the line,

*Chelsea, they were coming for you.*

I stop, silent. Wait. Repeat her words in my mind.

*I wouldn't let them.*

The receiver hangs loose in my hand and I flash back to their faces on the sidewalk. Hot eyes burning at me, challenging me to move, Delilah stepping in between us, taking blows that were meant for me.

My throat closes. My words fall short. Delilah had become the shield and sword of my days, watching over me, protecting me, knowing there are battles I can never win, fighting against forces I could never overtake. My breath passes across the receiver and I close my eyes. Her voice falls into my ear,

*You're my best friend. Now, you're all I've got.*

Delilah, my friend. Walking beside me, savior in arms, matching my steps, loving me when nobody else did. She deserves all I can give her—everything.

But the next day, when the alarm rings and the school bus honks outside of my driveway, I find myself telling Mama I can't go. I make up some symptoms, complain about my throat, my stomach—whatever will move her. She feels my forehead, palms my cheeks, looks into my eyes as I look away.

*Go back to bed, honey.*

I stay there for days— almost a whole week passes. I lay in my bed hour after hour, listening to my alarm radio, staring into the ceiling. I emerge from my bed for soup and hot tea. When Delilah calls each night, Mama places her hand over the receiver, her eyes move to mine and I shake my head, hold my stomach.

Soon, I find myself back at school in those early morning moments before the bell, standing in the window of the library, watching two stories below as Delilah waits at our morning meeting spot, the corner sidewalk. I see her scan the street for my car, *not knowing I asked Mama to drop me off behind the building.* I see her check her watch again and again. When the bell rings, she moves towards the doors, head down, face drawn-in.

At lunch, I eat alone outside on a bench, under the shade of a sycamore. I know she's looking for me, scanning the cafeteria line, looking into faces, asking people, *Have you seen Chelsea? Is she here? When did you see her last?*

I cannot move my feet to meet her, I can't draw my gaze to see her—whatever shame I carried before Delilah has been compounded by her love. I am too weak, too guilty to hold such love, and on this day, in the early spring when I am 14 years old, I deny her the love I'm so desperate to hold.

I break her heart and my own.

Days later at an assembly, I feel that familiar itch, of someone watching, someone thinking of me, and before I can stop myself, my eyes meet hers. Those brown eyes looking back at me from across the auditorium. Eyes that ask, *Why?* Eyes that beg me to return. I stare back for a moment, I offer no answers—I have none.

Weeks pass, and I no longer see her in the library window—some days, I no longer think to look. The corner sidewalk is empty. My heart fills with relief that she no longer expects me and simultaneous dread that our moments together have passed. And I know even if I swallow down that dread, pass the lump forming solid in my throat, even if I run out of this library and chase her through the locker-lined hallways and put my face in front of hers, I know there is too much I can't answer. Explanations I cannot give, feelings I do not have words for. I can only bring my trembling fingers to that windowsill, touch the cold glass, as my breath fogs against the image, covering over that empty sidewalk corner. There are things we surrender we can never get back.

She will return to that rough crowd, and they will take her back. Her time with me will seem like an odd vacation to a place she once knew, once loved, but in which she no longer resides. My name will fade from her lips, my memory will get tucked away, behind so many unanswered questions. The same questions that disturb our dreams, shake us out of sleep, trying to remember and trying to forget. Questions returning us to memory, trying to piece together things lost, things once had. And I too will return to the territory I know best. Always standing on the outside looking in, yearning for that friend I'm desperate to know, desperate to love but unable to keep.

Desiring to be the friend I could never be.

*Chelsea Schott is a literature teacher living in Texas. She holds a Bachelor's in American Literature and a Master's in Liberal Studies. A graduate of Rice University, she is president of the MLS Writers hosting workshops and speakers. You can find her writing in recent issues of* Germ Magazine, Under The Gum Tree *and the* Winter Tangerine Review.

# ON THE BACK STOOP

---

ANGELA AMMAN

We were too smart to smoke.

We did it anyway, lighting cigarettes from one flame and inhaling the immortality of the young with each clouded breath. We shook them from matching boxes, and when we decided to change brands we did it together. At night, when the dorm locked the outside doors, we stuck a lighter in the jamb so we wouldn't have to go through the trouble of walking to the front of the building after extinguishing our butts.

Cigarettes weren't the only things we shared. Index cards and highlighters and pages of notes scribbled in the basement study area ensured grades encased in steel. Even my French, which I struggled to understand let alone speak, bent to the pressure of conjugated verbs on flashcards and monotonous vocabulary quizzes. On Friday nights we smuggled beer or vodka into our dorm room, giggling over the confidence boosted by booze long before we realized we could find it within ourselves.

Our corner room offered perfect access to the side

stoop, and our cigarette breaks became more frequent. The dependence wasn't physical; what we craved were the revelatory moments we exhaled. Our friendship grew over those cigarettes—and my inability to say no to anything that might ruffle the smooth lines of our relationship.

On that back stoop I learned gossip became gospel when repeated with authority.

I inhaled acrid smoke in the fall air, clicking the lighter and staring at the flame instead of disagreeing when her words about mutual friends turned to vicious whispers. My head danced with the power of living away from home and of finding an ally with more ambition than scruples. Sarcasm and vitriol wove chains around our bond, my discomfort shoved into that compartment where we keep feelings we aren't ready to face. I buried shame and guilt and the knowledge that sometimes not disagreeing is just as damning as cutting down our friends with my own razor-sharp words.

My highlighters began to fade, and I bought more, savoring the stringent control over my class schedule. Slashes of color marked planner pages and syllabi; my roommate and I shared a table and lined up grades like little invisible trophies. We studied in our room sometimes, pop music seeping into the hallway, but in a world before Facebook we relished the study room table as a way to let everyone know exactly where we'd be most weeknights. Even when I didn't need to study, I dragged my binders down the stairs in my monogrammed messenger bag. I doodled in margins because it seemed ridiculous to chance my grades to take off a few nights—it seemed even more ridiculous to color outside the lines we'd started to carve around our friendship.

Routine held our spots at the table when we wandered to our back stoop for cigarette breaks. We slid single cigarettes and lighters from our bags, leaving the spoils of our study session strewn on the table. Dorms are filled with distractions and open doors, and we lingered in doorways to chat. I ignored inconsistencies in stories that unfolded in those doorways, the shift in personality that happened depending on which doorway was open on our walk outside. I ignored the inconsistencies between my thoughts and what tumbled out of my mouth—a potent mixture of sarcasm and uncertainty about how to temper it with grace. She reveled in the walk, her easy smile drawing in whoever happened upon it. That smile seemed contrived when I balanced it against the secrets we shared with our legs pressed against the rough concrete steps.

I learned her dad was sick on those steps. I hugged her, and lit another cigarette. I said all of the things I imagined a good friend would say, though I never believed anything bad would dare to land in her orbit. I agreed to everything after that, thinking I was offering support, not realizing I was filling the spaces between us with sand, waiting for wind.

I said yes to vodka Fridays and Saturdays, even as the niggling feeling grew that my alcohol tolerance would never match my enthusiasm. Walking to our familiar stoop meant stumbling a little those nights, and soon my own sarcastic barbs met hers in the middle. We whispered together, letting our laughter carry across the courtyard, and I pushed away the feeling that if she would say these things about people she'd known far longer and far more intimately than I, her words behind my back weren't likely very kind. But I lit cigarettes shaken from that blue and white box and kept whispering.

We went to parties, and I danced until my feet hurt. I talked myself into liking running shoes because she did and ignored how much I missed the heels gathering dust at the bottom of our shared closet. Our music tastes collided in the perfect way, and I let myself ride the notes of synchronicity into the belief that all of our thoughts could fit together the same way. We linked arms on our walk home, our heads together as we recounted who said what and why black party pants were ridiculous. I heard myself agreeing, while wondering where I could find a pair and would they look right on me and would I finally pull out the heels from the corner behind my laundry basket. Something like resentment emerged between us, but I kept whispering and nodding.

I don't remember when I started to feel the fissures that had been growing each time I said yes when I meant no.

Cigarette butts collected in the cracks in the sidewalk, even though we told anyone who'd listen that we threw most of them where they were supposed to be tossed. I talked until my voice hurt, until I was unsure which revelations were true and which parts simply a reflection of a person who seemed so much stronger than I felt. I nodded when she suggested I needed space from a boyfriend, though she seemed to be juggling two of her own fairly successfully.

I lit matches and watched the flames dance down the cardboard to my fingertips. Her dad was sick, and I listened to her words, but at some point I stopped believing they came from her heart. I listened and made promises to be there for her, always, whenever she needed, no questions asked. I told myself my words didn't count, because she wasn't being fair—not to the two guys waiting inside the dorm's doors. My dad wasn't sick, but when we're young we pull on self-righteousness without cause, and I unconsciously decided how she should be acting. My lips formed *yes* constantly, agreeing and smoothing, and I ground my teeth against the words I should have said.

Eventually, of course, I said *no*.

My friendship never wavered, not outwardly. I hugged and soothed; I pledged allegiance with one hand and checked the sorority rush schedule with the other. When she mentioned her dad's surgery date, she did it casually, as though my presence was guaranteed. Her offhand tone rankled; it made me feel small and unimportant, and I signed up for rush with a flourish, wanting something of my own.

She needed me. She didn't need someone to share a lighter twenty steps from the dorm room in which we would never smoke. She needed me to keep one of the billion promises I'd made between inhales and exhales. Her tone made me feel small because I was too angry about the wrong things to remember my presence seemed guaranteed because I'd never given her reason to doubt me. She needed me.

And I said no.

I shouted it, cosmically at least, the word echoing in the chasm between us that I'd let my silent resentment carve. I'd gathered the strength for that *no* for months, tucking it into corners every time I felt irritation at my silent acquiescence. I let it grow there, not understanding that nothing truly strong could grow in the darkness.

I said yes a million times I didn't have to—comments about friends and which way to walk home from a party and which song to listen to first on a car ride. But the first time she needed my yes, a sincere request for support, I sensed her weakness and attacked. I finally spat the no in her face the one time she needed me to say yes, and our friendship shattered against my cowardice.

We limped along for a time, our bond an echo of what it had once been. Now miles and years separate us beyond repair, yet I sometimes drift back to 19, and I wonder what would have happened if I would have said *no* long before it came out as a weapon instead of a word.

*Angela Amman is a short story and essay writer who lives in southeastern Michigan with her husband and children. She blogs at AngelaAmman.com, reviewing books and capturing the craziness and beauty that weave together to create something extraordinary. Angela is thrilled to share others' stories as a co-director/co-producer of Listen to Your Mother Metro Detroit. She is a managing editor at Bannering Books and contributing writer at AllParenting and Savvy Sassy Moms. Angela plans on running her fourth half-marathon this fall. She developed a running habit in college, the same year she writes about in her My Other Ex essay. When she should be sleeping, she works on her latest short story collection. Her short stories have appeared in her collection, Nothing Goes Away, and various anthologies.*

# THE GIRL WITH THE PINK BOW

ALETHEA KEHAS

It's the middle of winter and I'm hurling snow. Shovelfuls of the heavy wet stuff. I scoop and heave as my children glide their kid-sized shovels across the exposed pavement, pretending to help. We've been out here for 45 minutes, and we're all starting to get crabby and cold, but the driveway isn't finished and I won't stop until it is. Technically, I only need to clear a small space at the end so my husband can park his car safely off the road after work, and then later after he's eaten and the kids are in bed, he'll shovel the rest. Even though my husband doesn't mind shoveling, I don't want to leave the task I've started unfinished.

I'm tired, and the sweat dripping down my back is mixing with the icy flakes of snow that sneak past the collar of my jacket. Nearby, my three-year-old son and five-year-old daughter are no longer happily shoveling imaginary snow but each other into the expanding banks beside the driveway.

"Leave each other alone!" I yell between shovelfuls.

My children ignore me, continuing their battle in the snow.

"Go inside and watch TV! I'll be done in ten minutes," I tell them.

As I fling the last six feet of accumulated flakes in front of the garage, Ann appears. She's not literally here of course; I haven't seen Ann since I ran into her at L.L.Bean when we were in our early twenties. That last awkward encounter when we both pretended we were old childhood friends. Now, as I shovel the last clumps of snow from the driveway, I realize I am angry. That all of the buried hurt I endured when we were teenagers has caused me to feel this sudden, boiling of rage. The emotion of revenge is fleeting, but intense. The snow I am shoveling takes the form of Ann's body, and I dig the blade one final time into its white surface, flinging its heavy bulk over the bank. My heart slows as I put away the shovel and close the door to the garage, but my mind is reminding me that I'm still waiting for Ann to say, "I'm sorry."

I met Ann one sunny morning when we were in the fourth grade. My best friend Margot and I were playing double-dutch on the playground with two other girls, while we waited for the bell to ring to signal the start of the school day. It was impossible not to notice Ann strolling through the parking lot with the principal, as though she already belonged.

Walking our way was a girl we had never seen before, proudly sporting pink capris tied in bows below her knees and a matching vest. The outfit, I thought, was wonderful, but even better was the hat she wore on her head. This too matched, with its thick pink bow wrapped above a wide straw brim. No one in the fourth grade had a hat like that. How bold she was, I thought, as I watched her approach with an easy smile spread across her freckled face. Surely, she must have come from a bigger, more impressive town than ours.

She had, as she generously shared that first day on the playground. Like Margot, Ann was not shy. She answered with pleasure all of our questions about her past and present life, happy to be the center of our attention. Already I envied Ann's confidence, as I had often envied Margot's.

For the first few weeks after her arrival, everyone wanted to be Ann's best friend, including Margot and me. Margot had the advantage of having Ann in her classroom, but I did a good job of making up for lost time on the playground, in the cafeteria, and during weekend sleepovers.

Margot, Ann, and I took turns being best friends until we started junior high in a neighboring town. Then everything started to change, at least for me. After being overlooked by the boys from my hometown throughout most of elementary school, I was suddenly feeling both pretty and popular. A week rarely passed without a boy asking me to be his girlfriend, and I was invited to all the parties that mattered. As I immersed myself in this new, wonderful experience called junior high, Margot and Ann became less of a focus in my life. They, in turn, remained close.

The beginning of eighth grade was a lot like seventh grade. Boys were still asking me to be their girlfriend, and I spent more time talking on the phone than I did on my homework. Margot and Ann, who were again sharing a homeroom and sporting activities, were closer than ever, but I hardly noticed. That is, until they started dating Matt and Brian.

Matt and Brian were also best friends, but they were in the tenth grade. The two boys were not very popular among their peers, but the fact that they were in high school was all that really mattered to me and my classmates. Margot and Ann were soon proudly displaying Brian and Matt's class rings on their thumbs, and had won the envy of the eighth grade girls. We coveted their rings so much that some of us decided we also had to date boys from the tenth grade.

In more ways than one, I was pretty sure. While I had only gone as far as kissing boys, rumors were starting to circulate about Margot and Ann and what they were doing with their high school boyfriends. In the seventh grade, I had heard a tale about Margot and a boy from band class, but hadn't given it much thought until one day in the middle of the eighth grade.

I was eating lunch with my new best friend, Ellen, when I heard the lyrics from Led Zeppelin's "D'yer Mak'er" for the first time. The low, sexy notes rolled across the table and bumped uncomfortably into my ears. "Oh, oh, oh, oh, oh, oh, you don't have to go, oh, oh, oh, oh, oh." The singer was Ann, her unabashed voice luring our classmates into her pleasure.

"It's just like sex," I was certain I heard her say after she finished repeating her favorite line two more times.

"I know. It's the perfect sex song," Margot added with a knowing smile.

I peered down the length of the table at the two girls who were transforming into strangers behind my back. I imagined Margot with the boy from band class in the field beside her house. The dry, dusty grass-turned-hay separating their bodies, as Margot sat with her skirt hiked above her waist, her red panties parted to the side, moving to the gentle pulse of Led Zeppelin's song above a boy just fourteen. Margot and Ann, I was now convinced as I listened to them giggle and sing several seats away from me, were traveling the road of sex.

I wasn't ready to follow them, but I was willing to dance with Margot's boyfriend, Brian. The night of the school dance Margot was at her father's house for the weekend, but that didn't dissuade Brian from going without her. I wasn't dating anyone, so I went with Ellen who was more interested in cross-country running than in boys. Ellen looked inconspicuous in her jeans and t-shirt, but I was dressed to be noticed. My legs, shaved from the knees down, were bare under a jean miniskirt and I had on my favorite royal blue, three-quarter-sleeved blouse that matched the color of my eyes. I knew I looked good.

The first time Margot's boyfriend asked me to dance I hesitated.

"Oh, come on. It's no big deal. It's just a dance," he told me with a smile that should have made me turn away.

Instead, I let Brian's arms nestle into the curve of my back while the lyrics of Heart pulled our bodies together. When the music slowed a second time, and Margot's boyfriend began making his way across the dance floor, I noticed Ann's face framed in the shadows.

"You want to dance?" Brian asked again as though he had already forgotten the girl spending the weekend at her father's.

"I'm not sure that's a good idea," I said, nervously looking around for Ann.

The arms that wrapped around me had grown bolder,

and by the middle of the song their hands were resting on the rise of my butt.

"You look pretty tonight," Brian whispered in my ear. Ann, I saw, was watching us like a museum security guard while she danced in the arms of her boyfriend.

A third time he returned. It seemed this boy had no guilt, and in the moment after he asked me for another dance, I flirted with power. What if, I wondered, I gave him one more dance? If I let his skin feel mine through the shield of denim, would he go back to her? I didn't want Margot's boyfriend, though. In my eyes he was more annoying than cute, even in the muted light of the cafeteria. Besides, I was not the kind of girl who would deliberately steal something that didn't belong to me.

The Monday after the dance, I saw Margot with Brian, walking closely beside Ann and Matt. I knew I was in trouble. During the course of the day, whenever I crossed their path, Margot and Ann would sneer, whisper, and look away. By lunchtime I was sure the whispers that followed their gaze were directed at me. I knew Ann had told Margot about the dance, and in the mix of her words I had become the only one to blame.

On Tuesday, I opened my locker to find magazine cutouts of Rob Lowe and Tom Cruise defaced with black marker bearing the words "Cunt" and "Bitch." A quick rise of red spread across my features as I listened to my locker-mate catch her breath behind me. When I turned to look at her, she merely shook her head, gathered her books, and walked on down the hallway. I was crushed. This was a girl I considered my friend, a girl I had met in seventh grade and whom I had had over for a sleepover. She had slept in my bed while I slept on the bottom bunk that used to be my sister's. The next night, after my friend went home, I had pulled down the covers and crawled into my bed. My bare skin recoiled when it met the cool sensation of moisture. It could only be urine, I realized. Annoyed and embarrassed for my friend, I changed the bedding, but never mentioned her accident to anyone at school.

Now, standing alone by our locker, I felt wholly betrayed and alone. I wanted to vanish. Instead, I followed my classmates to science class. The snickers started in the front row, and followed the attendance cards to the back of the room where I was seated. The red that had not left my face was now searing. On the index card baring my name, the word "Smells" appeared in blue ink.

Faces now turned my way whenever I passed a group of students in the hallway. Eating lunch under the fluorescent glare of the cafeteria lights became nearly impossible. Through each steady drone of voices I was sure I could hear the whisper of my name. Laughter inevitably followed.

I hated going to school. Each morning I woke to the fear of what Margot and Ann might have in store for me that day. I was paranoid about rumors I knew where circulating about me. My long history with Margot had convinced me of her gift for fabrication and exaggeration. No one, though, cared to share what they were hearing about me, and I was too ashamed to ask. The realization that most boys were no longer asking me out, and the popular girls were now shunning my presence, was really all I needed to know.

It didn't take long for Brian and Matt to join their girlfriends in my humiliation.

"Hey Eamon, *Eamon!*" the middle name my birthfather gave the girl he wanted to be a boy, chased me down the hallway. It was a name I had tried to hide until it appeared printed in black ink on our sixth grade graduation program. Now everyone knew my embarrassing secret.

One day, I passed Margot and Ann on my way to math class. "Look, she's wearing a skirt again," they whispered to the students around them. "That means she's having her period." Somehow I got through the class and the rest of the day, but later, when I got home, I asked my mother if I could start wearing tampons.

Weeks laster, I stepped off the school bus, opened the metal door of our mailbox, and pulled out its contents. On the top of the envelopes addressed to my parents, there was a small rectangular package with my name on it. A spark of excitement traveled through my chest as I wondered about this unexpected surprise.

Alone in my bedroom, I tore through the brown paper to reveal an envelope on top of a white box. On the white surface I read the words, *Gentle Glide,* in pink italics. A flush of red filled my face as I opened the flap at the top of the container and removed one of the six cylinders encased in pearly white paper. The wrapper tore easily with the pull of my fingers, revealing a pink plastic tube. The tampons, I thought, were much nicer than the blunt-edged cardboard ones I'd just started to use.

It must be a promotional mailing, I thought, but my hands shook while I opened the letter that I would never be able to finish. The first words were nice. In fact they were so nice, they mocked me as I read answers to questions I had never asked. The author of the letter, a representative of the tampon company, thanked me for inquiring about their products, while politely explaining that it was perfectly safe to wear tampons overnight, for up to seven hours, and that yes, masturbation with a tampon was normal and okay. The white paper trembled with the shake of my hands, and its black words blurred with the water filling my eyes.

Is this what they were now telling people, I wondered, that I liked to masturbate with tampons? In a flash of anger, I imagined folding the letter back into an envelope with a simple note, *Here are the answers to the questions you were wondering about.* I considered adding the word *Slut* at the end before I licked the seal without a signature. In the darkness of night, I thought, I'd deliver the letter to Margot's mailbox.

Instead, I gathered the contents of my "gift" and presented it to my mother, who was melting lead onto colored glass in her studio. She placed the hot iron on its stand and looked into my burning face. My mother knew that I had interrupted her art to share another story about Margot and Ann. She looked angry and tired as she read through the contents of the letter.

"Those little bitches," she said after she finished.

Although I had chosen to share with my mother only a fraction of the humiliation I had endured during the past year, it was enough for her to know that my life at school had been ruined by my two former friends. When I was at home I was a mostly moody and despondent teenager, spending as much time as possible inside my bedroom. That day would be the first and only time in my memory that my mother would take action to defend me.

Standing beside her, I watched my mother pick up the phone and dial Margot's number. I waited with my breath held inside my trembling chest for the ring of her call to be answered. While my mother spoke with Margot's mother, I mentally filled in the words I imagined were coming through the speaker of the phone. There was a pause, too short, while Margot's mother abandoned her connection to find her daughter.

"Okay," I heard my mother's resigned reply before she hung up the phone. I had lost again. Margot, I discovered, decided it wasn't worth the effort to lie about what she had done, but that was it.

"Well, at least she admitted it," my mother told me as she dialed Ann's number.

Ann's mother took the stance of defensive denial. Just like her daughter, who had yet to learn that her best friend had already confessed. Ann pleaded innocence, and her mother accepted her plea before hanging up the phone.

"Well, I did what I could, Alethea," my mother told me. "Hopefully they'll stop harassing you now."

I waited for the apology from Margot and Ann, but I never got it. I waited for my life to go back to the way it was before the dance. Instead, I suffered the fate of silence. Margot and Ann stopped openly shaming me, but continued to treat me as though I was an Untouchable. I had gone from the top to the bottom of the social castes of junior high, and I couldn't figure out how to climb my way back up. Although their boyfriends no longer shouted "Eamon" down the hallways when I passed, the popular students were still shunning me. When I dared to look at Margot and Ann, their faces were smug and cruel.

I still couldn't walk down the halls at school without worrying that every whispered word was about me. I couldn't answer questions in class or converse with a group of people without blood rushing to cover my face in shame. Even today if I let my mind wonder too much about another person's thoughts, I can't hold a conversation without the familiar mask of red.

The day Margot and Ann's focus turned to another girl, I felt my paranoia begin to abate. We were now in the tenth grade, the three of us learning archery with our peers on the school grounds during gym class. While taking aim, I heard the loud whisper of Margot and Ann's voices, and instinctively turned from my focus on the bull's eye to see if their gazes were directed my way. I shot my arrow with a surge of relief; the two girls, it seemed, were concentrating on Alice, and in particular her ass. It was the only flaw they could find on her, and on that day Alice's behind was accentuated by tight white pants.

When it was Alice's turn to try her hand shooting at the large white circle, Ann and Margot started snickering again among their huddle of friends. Boys included.

"Look at her ass," one of them said. "It could be the target."

Everyone laughed. The boys, even though they all, no doubt, harbored secret crushes on Alice, as she was beautiful, joined in. While I watched, I felt the pang of pleasure that it wasn't just me. But I never forgot.

About four years after I imagined Ann's face in the snow, I joined Facebook. Even though I carefully selected the friends I would send requests to, and decided not to include my maiden name, Ann quickly found me. I let her friendship request sit for days, but the discomfort of looking at her face after all those years of trying to forget her, was more than I could bare. I hit "decline" and figured that would be the end of it.

Only it wasn't. After I rejected her friendship request, I couldn't get Ann out of my mind. It wasn't that I was angry anymore, not really. I was feeling the unsettled discomfort of a story in need of an ending. I wanted a resolution, so I decided I'd be the first to offer an apology.

I sent Ann a friendship request, followed by a private message. In a few words, I told her how I was still harboring the pain from our past, and that I was sorry for my initial rejection of her friendship request. Ann's reply was quick to arrive, and as I read her words I realized I was not the only one ready to lift the heavy anchor from our childhood.

"I apologize for any hurt I have caused you in the past… I look forward to a happy future," Ann concluded her message.

I released my breath and wrote the words, "All is forgiven."

*Alethea Kehas lives and writes in Bow, New Hampshire, where she shares a home with her husband, two children, two dogs and two cats. In 2008 she began to write her life stories in the form of a memoir,* A Girl Named Truth, *for which she is seeking publication. The story she contributed to this collection, "The Girl with the Pink Bow," was adapted from her manuscript, which together explore the themes of silence and truth. Alethea's healing and writing journey have led her to publications in various literary journals, including:* Complete Wellbeing, The Whirlwind Review, Airplane Reading, TouchPoetry *and* Emerge Literary Journal. *In 2012 she started her own business,* Inner Truth Healing, *where she devotes time and energy to helping adults and children heal and uncover their truths.*

# HOLDING HANDS WITH THE VILLAIN

ALLISON CARTER

I can tell you stories of beautiful, powerful female friendships in my life and how they changed me. I can tell you stories of raw pain when a friend inexplicably and suddenly ceased being interested in me.

But I can also tell you a story where I inexplicably and suddenly dumped a good friend. Don't be shocked. In fact, I ask you to think about it. Have you ever backed away from a female relationship? Has it been someone you knew loved you but you still walked away?

Being the one doing the dumping is just as hard as being on the receiving end. But what then? When we get dumped we fall on our support group, cry, have a glass of red wine, and mourn. How do you move on when you are the one who has caused pain and trauma to someone you really did love? No one holds your hand through that.

Have you been there before?

I am going to tell my story of the time I was the villain. I am going to tell you how I dumped my best friend. Maybe you can hold my hand afterwards, for ten years later it is still an open wound.

After graduating from college I moved to the big, wide world of the City. I moved to Washington, DC to pursue the life of…well… I don't know what I was looking for but I knew I wanted it to be exciting, fast paced, and full of adventure.

It turns out, though, that a city, no matter how smaller-than and lesser-than-NYC it is, can be terrifying. This is especially true when you move on your own, with no ties and no support to a place you can't afford. Above all, it can be terrifyingly lonely.

I was navigating city life, figuring out how much money I could spend going out to bars with my work colleagues while buying ramen for dinner, when I met a friend. A real, true, beautiful, kindred-spirit type of friend.

Her name was Bethany.

Two single Scorpios, the same age, both new to the city, we instantly bonded. We connected over our love of dance (taking classes in a hot, sweaty studio on the second story of an old house in Dupont Circle) and Broadway musicals.

True to our Scorpio nature we became friends in a fast and furious manner. My roommate at the time was contemplating a move out and I encouraged her so Bethany could move in. Bethany and I were going to take DC by storm.

My loneliness ebbed as I knew that Bethany and I would do everything, see everything, and share everything. We were together and unstoppable.

But you know the end of this story already. I dumped her.

No, we did not fight over a guy. Blissfully, Bethany and I had distinctly different tastes in men. She liked them unrefined while I, apparently, had a thing at the time for immaturity.

Eventually I fell into my signature, tumultuous City relationship. There was a man I, for some naïve and absurd reason I can only attribute to wanting to get new china and not share a bathroom with another woman ever again, thought I was going to marry. He dumped me. Suddenly, inexplicably. It was a hard and a jolting shock to my life plan. But Bethany held my hand, and I made it through, stronger.

That's when things changed.

After spending some time soothing my wounds with Ben & Jerry's ice cream, I was scarred yet decided to put myself back out there. This time, though, I had a self-confidence level that was at an all-time low.

I had no idea where I was going. I wanted to take new steps down that street that would lead towards lifetime satisfaction, that street that ended with a house holding my dream life behind its doors. But I had no idea which street that was. I was confused by the turns, roundabouts, and unnamed roads.

I eventually stumbled into a fantastic group of creative, unique, young professionals. I felt like I was moving in to the next phase of my life. I was moving away from "Sex and the City" and towards "Friends."

I did not want to take Bethany with me.

I don't know why. I loved her, she loved me, and we had been through so much together. I still enjoyed her company, but I was beginning to feel suffocated. I wanted something outside of her. I wanted to explore these beautiful, charismatic, funny people on my own, unfettered.

Things were changing between us. For example, although Bethany never asked, I felt obliged to drive back through the winding roads of Arlington, with the rush hour traffic, to pick her up to attend my kickball game. She didn't even play. I began to resent this.

*"I don't want a friendship like this anymore,"* I thought. I wanted to do things without her. It seemed that powerful female friendships can morph into something co-dependent very easily.

Did I talk with her about this?

No. I was a jerk instead.

The truth is I was really confused. I was stuck in a cocoon so tight I didn't know if I would ever make it out, let alone emerge, having conquered the changes I was facing. I wanted to know who I was, where I stood, and my place in the world. Bethany bore the brunt of my confusion.

Things disintegrated farther at one of my kickball games. She was watching me and my newfound friends play (having declined to join the team). The team and I were having issues trying to determine where to put our keys and wallets, while we played on a rather rough-looking field in Adams Morgan.

Bethany collected all of our personal items and stood in one spot for the entire game, being a proud steward of our valuable belongings.

This broke me.

*"We don't need a team mom!"* I thought to myself. *"What is she doing? Why is she here?!"*

It never occurred to me that she was there because of me. Or that she was there because she was just as desperate to have new, beautiful, charismatic, funny friends in her life as I was. I couldn't see past my indignation on her behalf (she was too good to be treated like a team mom to peers) and my indignation on my own behalf (I just wanted to be alone in this new crowd).

I became aware of how we had become completely immersed in each other's lives. I knew then I wanted out, even if that meant playing kickball while jangling my own car keys into second base.

I backed away. Slowly, cowardly. I started sneaking around, not telling her what party I was going to, and lying about the friends I met downtown for lunch. I knew at the time what I was doing was wrong, and I felt guilty. But I didn't stop either. I have never cheated on a boyfriend. Yet I was clearly cheating on my best friend, my friend who did nothing wrong.

Eventually, as it was bound to, the ticking bomb of our friendship exploded. I was at work, at a new job I was thrilled to have. After struggling to find my calling, to find a job that didn't incite panic attacks every morning at 8 a.m., I was getting to a happier, more confident place. I believed I had found that road to my dream life, even if I hadn't walked all the way down it yet.

Then Bethany called me at my office one morning.

"Why don't you like me anymore?" she immediately launched. "What have I done to you?"

She was so achingly sad. Her heart was broken, she felt abused and betrayed. I had taken our precious friendship and, for reasons she didn't know, smashed it. I gave her no warning, I was not careful or gentle with her love, and I abandoned the years of our friendship without even trying to reshape it first.

Her pain made me angrier. The beast in me appeared

and all the rage I felt at the world and that ex-boyfriend came boiling out.

"I just don't understand why you can't get a life of your own! I can't carry you all the time! We need to be independent, I need to be free! You are smothering me! I just can't do this anymore."

I said more things, none of them worth remembering. I have never said these things to an ex-boyfriend yet Bethany heard them all. At this point she was sobbing, as I was shaking and yelling. I was ugly. So ugly.

Things didn't end with hugs and a new level of understanding. I slammed the phone down and returned to my work, frustrated. Most of that frustration was with myself for losing control and for saying things I didn't mean.

Where had that come from? Why couldn't I be a nicer person? Why was I just so wicked to someone who loved me so much?

My new boss had the office next door. Five minutes after I slammed down the phone and pounded on my keyboard like I was urgently sending wartime telegrams, he knocked on the door I had closed before the phone call.

"Hey, you okay?" he said.

"Yes, I'm fine," came my stock reply. I paused, "Why do you ask?"

"Well, that sounded like a really bad break up."

Yes. It was.

Bethany moved out pretty quickly after that. We didn't keep in touch. My birthday party photos immediately following this show no trace of her, not even in the background.

Every time I think of her I am filled with regret. I wish

I could go back ten years, hold her hand, and tell her what I was going through. I wish I had given her a chance to help me. I wish I had explained to her that I was a steam engine with a load of coal that just needed to be burned and I was ready to pummel anyone on the tracks, even if they opened their arms to hug me. I wish, I wish, I wish...

I wish I could call her today. I wish I could hear her voice and tell her all of these things. I have held on to these secrets, these feelings, this remorse. I wish I had the courage to find her and tell her that she was a wonderful person.

I know our relationship was headed down a co-dependency path. I am aware that my need for independence had to be honored. But I also know I should have attempted to create a new kind of friendship, instead of hiding, cheating, lying, and yelling. I could have found the road to my new life and let her walk with me part of the way.

They say time heals all wounds, but I don't believe it; my wounds are not healed. I took the love of a beautiful, strong, funny, talented woman and smashed it heartlessly.

I hope she knows how much she meant to me. I hope she knows I still remember our antics.

And I hope she knows how very, very sorry I am and that her story, our story, is in my heart forever.

*Allison Carter lives in Chapel Hill and is a content strategist and writer for companies (see that element of her life at allisonbcarter.com), but her heart is in her creative career. She blogs regularly at Go Dansker Mom (http://godanskermom.com) on anything and everything that modern moms think about. Her pieces have appeared on* Scary Mommy, What the Flicka?, mom365, Mampedia, *and in the book* The Her Stories Project *as well as in various local news outlets. She loves to speak professionally, too, having last been seen at the Digital Marketing for Business Conference.*

# JESSIE'S GIRL(FRIEND)

SHANNAN YOUNGER

The moment I met Jessie is one of my earliest memories. It was the first day of Kindergarten and we were at recess. There were two ways to get to the top of what seemed like the gigantic slide on the playground equipment. Another little girl and I had started from opposite sides and reached the summit at the same time.

First, I admired how pretty she was. With bright blue eyes and shining blonde hair with a little curl to it, she looked like those perfect girls portrayed in the picture books I read at home. Then, I panicked. What did one do in this situation? How in the world did we decide who would go first?

Jessie broke the awkward silence.

"You can go first," she said softly.

I vividly remember feeling several different emotions.

The primary feeling was relief. The confounding social situation was solved. Phew! I was also pleased, because I really did want to go down that slide first. I felt enlightened, too. Kindergarten held the often mentioned promise of new friends, but I had been unclear on how one actually made those friends. This was my five-year-old "Aha!" moment. And I was intrigued. Why was this girl so nice? Where did she get her social savvy? Would she teach me?

I waited for her at the end of the slide and she smiled when she had finished whooshing down it. That's the extent of the memory; the details get blurry after that.

I'm not sure quite what happened next, but we ended up spending the rest of recess and the next nine years together.

We were best friends.

We played at each other's homes often. We ate lunch together and we spent many, many more recesses together.

One common quality Jessie and I shared was that we were not the most athletically gifted kids in our grade. No one was asking us to join the kickball team. Every now and then we'd try, but a ball to the face would send us back to the safety of the swings, chatting as we swayed. We also thought it was awesome that we shared the same middle name. That alone was enough to bond us for what we thought would be forever.

We were quite different, though that wasn't an issue. She was artistic, quiet, and laid back. I admired that she won all the coloring contests in Miss Fishbaugh's first grade class and ribbons at the county fair a few years later.

I, on the other hand, was not laid back, even in early elementary school. I was louder and far more interested in school than she was.

We balanced each other quite nicely. I didn't realize at

the time that I was living the meaning of yin and yang and the beauty that comes with that in a friendship.

There were different markers of our friendship as we grew up. Jessie was the lucky girl in our grade who got to host the first birthday party sleepover.

The excitement of being invited far trumped the fear of sleeping somewhere other than my own bed, until it was actually bedtime. Then, terror. As all the little girls examined the floor of Jessie's bedroom and started wondering about the logistics of sleeping, all eyes eventually turned toward Jessie's full size bed.

A hush fell over the crowd as we all realized that there was room for not just Jessie, but one other guest to join her.

I was the chosen one.

Again, sweet relief washed over me as fear left my body and gratitude for both friendship and a mattress replaced it.

Jessie always made me feel special, and I hope I did the same for her. My parties were smaller and not sleepovers, but I remember her there, front and center. She was my favorite and I was hers.

When I moved to a new home a mile away in fifth grade, most friends at my old school considered that to be an obvious cause for a breakup. Many of them said as much.

"Uh, we don't go to the same school any more so we can't be friends."

Jessie didn't do that. We remained friends, though less close without the daily classroom contact.

A year later we were together again in middle school and picked up right where we left off, mostly. Perhaps that incredibly tight bond was a little looser. There was more room for the many new people in school, and boys, and our different interests. Jessie wasn't about to join the Science Olympiad Team like I had, a wise social move on her part, and I certainly wasn't talented enough to be taking extra art classes.

Our friendship seemed somehow to be removed from a lot of the middle school drama, and I loved that being her partner in crime seemed easier than friendships with the other girls. We moved in different circles and that was okay. I think we provided a respite for each other from the usual tween angst. We were even able to handle each other's family dynamics, going so far as to travel together on spring break in seventh grade.

Eighth grade was a big year for us. She introduced me to the brave new world of boy bands. Specifically, my parents had her to thank for the fact that my room would soon be covered in posters of "New Kids on the Block." She even talked me into participating in a New Kids lip-syncing contest held at a bowling alley and aired on local access cable. I remember my mom asking me just why I thought this was a good thing to do. I told her, "Because Jessie's doing it."

Sitting next to Jessie in Mrs. Morrow's pre-algebra class was a highlight of my school day and fun for writing notes. When she busted out of her backpack a five-inch New Kids pin with an easel back and set it up on her desk, I was in awe. It had never occurred to me that such an item existed, nor that it was possible to bring Joey McIntyre to math class. I watched as Mrs. Morrow raised an eyebrow and went on with class.

I quickly followed suit. When I erected my button, Mrs. Morrow sighed and slightly shook her head, and then dove headlong into the world of variables, which I never understood.

Little did I know that variables, in a different yet similarly incomprehensible way, would come into play in our own relationship. It turns out that neither nine years of friendship nor the shared love of Donny, Danny, Jordan, Joey, and Jonathan were enough to keep us together.

At the end of eighth grade, I tried out for and made the high school band's flag corps. Band camp and practice took up a large chunk of my summer and I don't remember seeing Jessie much, if at all.

And then high school began. I scanned the hallways for her, but didn't find her. The rivers of people flowing between classes were full of new faces, none of them Jessie's.

When I did eventually find her, she was different. Aloof. I think we tried to talk but had nothing to discuss.

Soon, she was unrecognizable to me. Literally. I had gone the way of the band geeks, and Jessie had become a goth, wearing all black and a heavy eyeliner that I would not have known how to apply even if my parents had been okay with it. She dyed her shining blonde hair jet black.

The Jessie I knew was gone. Just like that, with the start of high school, our friendship was over. We were doomed by the new social structure and the death knell was sounded. We didn't have another significant conversation again.

Maybe I was waiting for her to be the one to know what to do, as she did in Kindergarten. But she never made a move, and neither did I.

I often wondered what happened.

High school happened. Different interests happened. Cliques happened.

And I let them happen. But it seems like somehow there's more to it than that, although I've never been able to pinpoint what. I let the friendship slip away. I didn't understand the goths and frankly was a bit afraid of them, all dark and trench-coated and seemingly closed-off. Our differences, which had never been a problem before, were now insurmountable.

I don't know why I didn't just call her. I'm sorry I never reached out. I don't know why I didn't have the fortitude to buck the social system and sit with her at lunch, or why she passed me in the hallways without a word or sign of recognition.

It was so odd to see her in the hallways time and time again and be complete strangers, as if the previous nine years had never happened.

We were in the same English class senior year and our assigned seats at opposite ends of the classroom seemed symbolic. She was always late, and many days when I saw her enter after the class was well underway, I would wonder what had happened. I would stare at her, searching for signs of the best friend I had loved not that long ago. Sadly, I found nothing.

We graduated and both of us moved away, as did my parents, so I rarely make it back to our hometown. I've heard that Jessie goes by her middle name now, and works at a salon.

Her profession doesn't surprise me. My mother has a photograph of me that she took after Jessie had given me a makeover at age 12. She had done my hair and made it big and curly. For years I had tried and failed to achieve that look, and she made it happen in a matter of minutes. She did my makeup and I looked like myself, but different. I remember that when Jessie revealed my makeover to me in the bathroom mirror, I felt like I was back at the top of that playground slide. I wondered where she had acquired her knowledge, a question I always had about her, and I was grateful for her ability to make me feel special.

Every now and then I think about trying to connect with her, but my efforts to find her on social media have been unsuccessful. Even if I did find her, I'm not sure what I would say or how it would be received. So I simply remain grateful for the nine years of childhood friendship that we shared.

*Shannan Ball Younger is a blogger and freelance journalist who writes about parenting and the laughter and tears that come with it on the blog* Mom Factually, ChicagoNow's Tween Us *blog, and* Chicago Parent *magazine. You can also find her work in* The HerStories Project's *first book, on* Mamapedia *and in* Make It Better Magazine. *Shannan was also a part of the 2013 Chicago cast of* Listen To Your Mother. *Originally from Ohio, she is a recovering attorney living in the Chicago suburbs with her husband and daughter.*

# FUCHSIA

CATHERINE CARSON

The last time I saw Megan, she wore a fuchsia bra. I told her I couldn't be her friend unless she got some help, and I loved her.

I'd met Megan while setting up my dorm room freshman year. I walked through our shared bathroom to find her in a blue bathrobe, hanging a picture above her bed. It was hand-drawn, an outline of someone with blue shading below the eyes. Later, I would learn that this was Megan's perspective of herself in the hospital in which she'd spent time for a heart problem.

I really don't remember what we talked about that day, but I remember that my heart beat fast. Like many other people, I was determined to make a new start at college, where no one knew me. High school hadn't been bad—I'd been drum major of my high school marching band for three years, I'd taken Advanced Placement classes, and I'd been supported by my favorite teacher to pursue a degree in English. However, I'd had mood issues and bad acne, and medication had caused me to gain thirty pounds, lose fifteen, gain twenty, and so forth. The summer before college, I met a man eight years older than me and fell deeply under a spell of unrequited love. I lost thirty pounds. This was very important to me. Size six pants hung off my hips, and the sparkly, blue spaghetti-strapped top I wore while moving into the college dorm that day showed off the area between my belly button and my midriff. This was the kind of outfit that normally prompted my dad to tell me to put on some clothes, but he'd said nothing about it that day.

Tired from moving, I met Megan, her blonde hair in a ponytail. Her tiny niche of a closet was stuffed with clothing, some exact replicas of other pieces, just in different colors, silver/gold, red/pink. Under her bed were boxes of clothes, too. "I bought size fours just in case I gained the freshman fifteen," she said.

My own closet held about six outfits. I was going to shop to build my wardrobe. I was going to see what was cool in college, and Megan was going to help me. When I dumped $250 at the mall, she dropped $500. When I spent $300, she spent $600.

Eventually, she asked me to lock her credit card in my lock box.

The details of our relationship spark up in my memory without a clear sequence. I don't remember how one thing led to the next. Here's what I do remember: She once woke me from a nap by singing "You Are Beautiful" by Christina Auguilera into a hairbrush. She screamed a lot when she was excited. We stayed up until 3:00am because she was trying to teach me to dance, to no avail. She looked in the mirror and poked at her abs. She could usually be found putting on makeup in front of her computer, and the speakers constantly dinged with the sounds of incoming instant messages, sounds that echoed through the wall and into my own bedroom, keeping me from sleep. She dated many boys, switching from wearing a Star of David to a cross, depending on who she was dating.

Our indoor uniform was pajamas. I borrowed a pair of her scrub pants. She had many because she'd been in the hospital so much with her heart condition.

Outside the dorm—at the mall, in the school's cafeteria, or in class—we wore shirts emblazoned with the logos of popular teen fashion stores, tight jeans, and layers of makeup.

One day, she lost track of a boyfriend. She called his dorm and cell phone and eventually rushed to his room, looking for him, crying. His roommate hugged her too long.

Back in her room, she said, "Let's go to Wendy's." We ordered hamburgers, fries, and two Frostys each. I couldn't believe we were eating it all, but we were. We started on the Frostys in my car and finished the meals in her room. We finished every last bite, every last spoonful.

I left to wash the grease off of my hands in my bedroom—we had separate sinks while the shared bathroom held only a shower and toilet. She said she was going to take a shower. The water ran, and the vomiting started. Tears came to my eyes. I understood what was happening, that this was the bulimia I'd learned of in TV dramas and freshman orientation.

I understood the psychological workings of this disease on a surface level. When I'd struggled with losing weight my senior year and over the summer, I'd run four miles a day, eaten as little as I could, made sure that what I did eat was as full of fiber as possible, and had attempted, when I was angry with myself, to vomit. But to no avail.

Weeks after I heard Megan in the bathroom, I tried vomiting myself, but I just couldn't physically do it. Instead, I counted hours between meals, dizzy and angry at the world. Twelve hours was my goal every day. And this wasn't good enough.

When I got bored with my clothes, I wore hers, my breasts stretching the fabric. She taught me the glory of sparkly G-strings and silky thongs, which I wore under short skirts when I accompanied her to Catholic Church services on campus. I was Episcopalian, not Catholic, but I wanted to be with her.

September 11th occurred, that big day of fire and stomachaches, of canceled classes and vigils in the student union. Every TV played footage, most notably the view from some tourist's video camera bouncing backward and upside-down, showing dust, fire, and shoes.

That's why we started going to church. I had unraveled. I'd called that guy I'd been in love with over the summer. "I'm glad you're okay," I said, even though he was in Florida, too, only 120 miles away.

I stared at my blue comforter, pressing my thumbnail into every stitch in the curving pattern. Alone, I watched *When a Man Loves a Woman* and cried and cried and cried.

Boys liked Megan. They leaned over me to kiss her. One day, a different boy didn't call her back right away about a date she desperately wanted to go on that night.

We went to the grocery store, bought a chocolate cake and love cards for ourselves, three each. We giggled while we cut thick slices in her room. She lay down for a nap, and I went to my room to do homework.

Eventually, I headed to the bathroom. There, I pushed

the door to, but not all the way closed, as the light in her room was out, and I was in a hurry. She rushed in, her pink shorts unbuttoned, black bra against pale skin. "He's here! He called and took me out for steak. He's here!" She squealed this nearly silently. In the bed on the opposite side of the dark room, I thought I saw something move.

I had leaned forward, covering my crotch with my shirt. "Good! Go, go," I said. She turned around, hair flying. I closed the door behind her as quietly as I could. When I returned to my room, I turned up my music and cried.

I didn't break up with her because of that. Boys loving her was not her fault. I didn't break up with her after the horrible weekend at her house, either.

She and I were headed to her family's house, about three hours away, for a weekend. "My brothers will love you," she said. "Bring a bikini."

Then, I learned that she'd invited Joey. "I don't want to go anymore," I said. "You and Joey go."

"But I need you to go! You're the whole reason I set up this trip in the first place."

And so I went.

We listened to Britney Spears' "I'm a Slave for You" on repeat on the way there. I hated that song. All I could think of was Spears with that python draped over her shoulders, the way she gyrated with that stupid microphone wrapped around her head, not to mention the horrible message of the song, that she was just a slave to some man, that she needed him for everything. I couldn't help but wonder, though, if I wasn't being defensive because there was no one in my life for whom to be a slave.

I sat in the back seat of Joey's Volkswagen. I wanted to vomit for the whole three-hour drive.

The house was teeming with boys. Spaghetti was served. The next day Megan, Joey, and I went shopping, and before that, Joey watched us perform what had become our makeup ritual in the bathroom near her childhood bedroom. "My mom will freak out if you get makeup on the counter," Megan said, so she dampened a washcloth and wiped away the trail of creamy foundation and pink powder we'd left in our wake.

There was a huge sale at Banana Republic, and, as usual, J. Crew called to us. At Express, I fit into the tiniest jeans I'd ever squeezed myself into.

"How do I look?" I asked Joey, who sat on a bench outside the dressing room.

He glanced my way. "Fine." Then Megan emerged from her room in her jeans, and we both rushed to her.

"How do mine look?" I asked.

"You look amazing," Joey said.

"Yeah, the color of the denim is cool," I said. They looked like clay. Both of us bought the jeans we'd tried on.

When we got back to her house, she insisted I hold her shopping bags. "Don't let my parents think they're mine," she said.

We swam with Megan's four brothers, and, as she promised, we played Marco Polo and the teenaged boys' wet fingers grazed my slippery skin. I smiled and laughed.

That night, the three of us hung out in Megan's bedroom. We turned on *An American Tail*, a tape found under Megan's bed, and we laughed, but the split-apart family of mice and that "Somewhere Out There" song got to me.

I fell asleep. I woke up to something, a flash, like that of a camera. In a state of half-sleep, I saw Megan and Joey kissing next to me, over the sheets and in the dark. His hands were up her shirt, unclasping her bra. She stood and shimmied out of it, t-shirt still in place, and then settled beneath him again.

I felt sicker than I had on the drive over, more unsettled than I had when I heard Megan throw up.

Into the bathroom I slipped. There, I cut myself for the first time.

There was no mess on the white tile. The thin lines from my razor's quadruple blades smarted, but I think only one bled. I'd reached to the back of my leg and swiped, and with the pain a new sensation rushed over me, not quite erasing the resentment I felt toward Megan or the shame I felt toward myself. I was still angry and then ashamed, even embarrassed, though no one knew what I'd done. For a euphoric instant, I felt relief, the way a stone must feel in the air between two skips, but then, like that stone, I fell into a place that was new and scary. Many people lost their virginity around my age of eighteen; instead, I cut.

As we drove by the ocean the next day, I imagined salt water against the pink lines on my leg, stinging. My new jeans were tight against my thighs. I regretted everything.

I told Megan the truth about cutting a few weeks later. I didn't mention the make-out, though. She encouraged me to go to the counseling center. There was more vomiting when the shower ran. I cried more. I wore her freshman-fifteen clothes.

Buttons and grommets dug into my skin. Secretly, I was glad my breasts were bigger than hers; the opening of an extra button at the top of a V-neck meant something to me.

Maybe that was the other side of not being able to vomit.

Megan or I—honestly, I can't remember which of us (sometimes it's that way with friends)—told a couple other girls in the dorm about my cutting, and the three of them walked through the bathroom and into my room one day.

"This is an intervention," Megan said.

"I'm not on drugs."

"We care about you." Megan's eyes were wide, and she spoke fast. I couldn't help but wonder what she got out of the drama, as I'll admit that as embarrassing as it was to call the university's counseling center in front of them, part of me enjoyed the attention.

That's not why I broke up with her.

I broke up with her because I met someone else. I spent time in the common area with my headphones on, Lisa Loeb blasting memories from that summer into my ears, and I waited, the way one might wait at a bar or coffee shop for that special person to walk through the door.

Meredith, who lived across the hall, had been going through her own issues, hers surrounding an abusive ex-boyfriend, and she joined me in the common area when she was home. We ran circles around campus together. She ate peanut butter out of the jar.

We sat in the common area and folded our underwear together. She had bright red hair and green eyes.

"You're hanging out with that weird girl?" Megan asked one day. "Yeah, she's cool. You'd probably like her."

She didn't. She drifted from me, hanging out with the other girls from the dorm and shooting me looks when she walked by and caught Meredith and me talking.

I knew they were talking about me. I'd talked about her

behind her back, too, when we were friends, under the guise of being worried about her bulimia, but possibly also because I wanted to fit in with everyone. I wanted to be everyone's friend, and I thought that sometimes you had to sacrifice your own reputation as a good person in order to do that.

Before entering her bedroom, I knocked on the bathroom door. This was not normal. She must have known something was up.

She didn't look at me. I don't remember what she was doing, but I do remember that she wore a fuchsia bra.

I said, "I think you need help."

She said, "It's my heart. My medication makes me throw up."

I paused. "Yeah. I'm worried."

Silence.

"I have to separate myself. I can't do this," I said. What I really wanted to say, though, was *Stop. I'm not safe with or without you.*

These were typical break-up words, but I didn't know that. I'd never broken up with a friend, had never had a boyfriend with whom to break up.

I didn't have the words, but I wanted to thank her. For everything.

She didn't look up at me. I left the room without closing the bathroom door, without being the first to make a sound.

After that year, I never saw her again. Twelve years later, I often wonder what seeing her would be like, what she'd look like now, and what, if anything, I would say. I wouldn't want to thank her. I'd want to show her who I'd become, how far I'd come into myself.

I know the truth, though: I'd sink again. I'd suck in my

breath while she looked me up and down. I'd look at her the same way, wondering if she still threw up with the shower running.

I wonder how much I hurt Megan by enabling her, stirring drama, and craving my own brand of attention. I wonder if, after I told her about the cutting, she drew a sharp breath of her own when she heard me enter the bathroom, just as I did when I heard the shower's knob squeak and the water flow.

*Catherine Carson teaches creative writing at Full Sail University in Winter Park, FL. She has served as Managing Editor of* The Florida Review *and has poetry forthcoming in* Referential Magazine. *She predominantly writes nonfiction, but she also enjoys a good pantoum now and then. Catherine was raised near award-winning sand in Sarasota, Florida. She is a fifth-generation Floridian who probably wouldn't know better than to wear flip-flops in the snow. She now lives in Central Florida with two cats who sincerely believe they are superior to her in every way. Swimming and cycling are her favorite past-times, and she will do anything to avoid cooking for herself.*

# WHEN WE'RE GROWN UP

# I CAN'T RELATE TO PIXIES

LEAH VIDAL

I felt my phone vibrate and a quick glance revealed that I had a new message on Facebook. Someone had commented on a recent photo I had posted. "I have you on my mind today." I stared at the screen. Seven words that at one time would have had me reaching for the phone. Seven words that now stirred up feelings of uncertainty and memories I thought I had laid to rest.

I had started a new job even though it wasn't the best time in my career to do so. I had a newborn, our first child. I don't recommend making any life-changing decisions when you are still trying to figure out how to balance the career you've worked so hard for and the dream you've finally realized—that of starting a family. No one warns you how you'll have to juggle the same deadlines, put in the same hours, show the same level of enthusiasm, and wow your bosses all on just a couple of hours of sleep. This is hard enough to do somewhere you've already proven yourself. It is nearly impossible to do when you're the new kid on the block.

After years of being a poster child for Corporate America, climbing the ladder at record speed, working full-time and pursuing a business degree simultaneously (I took my last final exam three days before my daughter was born), I no longer felt that drive and I didn't love the company I was now working for. Looking back, I understand it was partly due to being a new mom. But I can also see clearly now the company culture wasn't the right fit for me. And yet, I kept trekking along for lack of other options or the energy to devise a different career path.

"Hey, I'm Andie." I looked up from my desk to see what can only be described as a pixie. The kind that flitters from tree to tree, glowing in light, bright smile in place. It was possible the fairy tales I had spent so many evenings reading to my five-month-old daughter were getting to me, but I swear all I could wonder when I saw her was what this little pixie was doing in my office. "I'm new here and trying to find Human Resources. I'm supposed to get my badge photo taken though I'm not having the best hair day." The words tumbled out of her mouth with an energy my morning latte hadn't provided in many a week.

Bad hair day? Her pixie cut (yes, even her hair was like that of a nymph) looked perfect. I hadn't seen a good hair day, or stylist for that matter, in …how long had it been? I realized I had no idea when I had last stepped foot in a salon. I made a mental note to make an appointment. Her next question interrupted my thoughts. "Would you like to grab lunch later?" Something else I hadn't done in some time. I had resorted to eating at my desk in hopes of impressing the new boss and assuaging the guilt I felt for the few times I had arrived late or left a bit early due to my new motherly duties.

"Sure," I replied and found myself smiling back at her.

Lunch was only an hour long, but in that hour we covered years of our lives. By the end of those sixty minutes, we were the best of friends. I felt like not only did I know her on a deeper level, but also the teenage daughter she had raised as a single mother. She was younger than I was but had somehow experienced more. We were two women thrown together at different stages of our lives, each with our own once-upon-a-time and chapters yet to be written. After that day, we spent many lunch hours together, grabbed many cups of coffee together, and eventually started spending many weekends together.

As we delved deeper into our friendship, I learned my pixie friend wasn't all light. There was a darkness to her, deeply rooted in childhood experiences and life events that could cast a shadow on even the brightest of lights. I listened to her history, always supportive, always expressing my sympathy, but never being able to truly relate, as I had not experienced anything remotely similar to what she had been through. As tumultuous as her past was, I soon saw her present was beautiful chaos—she was passionate about life and a hopeless romantic. There were many late night phone calls seeking dating or relationship advice and I was happy to hash out the latest drama with her. One thing Andie never had a problem with was attracting a man. People of both genders were immediately drawn to her.

Two years after she floated into my office and ultimately my life, my husband was offered a position that required us to relocate three hours away from where we were currently living. Andie and I continued our friendship. She came to visit often and we even asked her to be our second child's godmother. With two young children now, I could no longer drop everything when the phone rang and sit and ruminate about Andie's most recent dating adventure. And, I soon began to realize just how unbalanced our friendship was from the beginning.

It seemed I gave a lot more than I received in our relationship, although Andie didn't quite see things that way. Our conversations were always more about what was going on with her than what was going on with me. With the same fervor I was initially drawn to, she would jump right into a phone call describing her latest dilemma without so much as a "How is your day going?" It hurt that my day wasn't important to her. I realized changing dirty diapers, enduring sleepless nights, and being the new mom in town weren't as exciting as the corporate deadlines and boss issues we once shared, but it was still my life.

Then came the phone call I believe was the beginning of the end of our friendship. My mom had just arrived to watch the kids so my husband and I could head out to celebrate our wedding anniversary for a few days. The phone rang and it was Andie...she was in tears. The tears were nothing out of the ordinary for Andie so I didn't immediately key in to the gravity of her news. She had found a lump in her breast; the doctor wanted to remove it and perform a biopsy to determine if it was benign or malignant. Her mother wasn't going to be there. Neither was her sister. She didn't want to go through it alone. She begged me to come. I replaced the receiver and told my husband what she had asked of me, and his response was instant, "You have to go and be with her. She can't go through it alone." I cancelled my romantic anniversary trip and headed right out to be with her.

As soon as I saw her, I could tell my little pixie was nervous, fluttering about a bit more than usual, talking a bit faster than normal. I was glad I had decided to come to her. I wouldn't want to face the medical unknown by myself. No one should. Except that shortly after I arrived Andie casually mentioned that her mom was coming and her sister too. The next morning as I sat in the waiting room of the hospital, family member after family member trickled in, and I seemed out of place, unnecessary really. I hadn't been the one to go back in the room with her, nor was I the one who was called in when the procedure was over.

The truth is, I wasn't a family member and didn't expect to play that role but with this much support, I also wasn't needed at the hospital. I slowly started to doubt my decision to cancel my trip. I told myself I would be useful to her once everyone left and Andie and I were back in her apartment. She would need help and support there and that must've been what she was thinking when she begged me to come.

When we arrived at the apartment, however, Andie's mom and sister set up shop and moved in for the night. They fussed over Andie and took very good care of her, expressing a bedside manner that surprised me from two people Andie had always described as cold and emotionally unavailable. It was heartwarming to see, but once again I realized there was no need for me to be there.

The next morning, Andie's mom and sister headed back home, leaving Andie and me alone. We lay on her couch, watched movies, talked, talked, and talked some more. When it was time for me to leave, Andie hugged me tight and told me it meant a lot to her for me to be there. She said she never truly expected her family to be as supportive as they had been, but she knew she could count on me. In that moment, I was glad to have made the decision to be there for my good friend. I wasn't accustomed to expecting the worst out of people like my dark pixie was prone to do, and I was grateful to have shone a bit of hope in her world.

Months passed and Andie and I remained close, although I started to pick up on comments she dropped here and there.

"Ever since we stopped working together, I feel like our dynamic has changed. It's like we can't really relate to each other."

"It must be so nice to have a husband to support you so you no longer have to work. I wish I had someone. Well, you can't relate to what it's like to be alone."

"I've been through so much in my past and worked hard to get to where I am today. I'm so tired of life throwing me curve balls. Well, you couldn't possibly relate to that. Your life has been perfect."

I ignored the comments, telling myself I shouldn't take them personally. They stemmed from her own issues, and the fact was I actually felt sorry for her. However, while I never addressed the comments I also stopped sharing parts of my life with her. I'm not sure if it was out of embarrassment or to avoid such comments in the future. Either way, our phone calls became few and far between.

A few months later, I had to have a hysterectomy and ended up with complications from which it took me ten weeks to recover. My mom flew in to help me with the kids, local friends pitched in, and my husband was supportive as always. Only one person never showed up, never called to see how I was feeling…Andie.

As I sit here telling this story, another notification

comes through on my phone. Andie's latest FB status: "Sadly, I am FIRMLY DISCONNECTING from a friend of 10 years. It breaks my heart that I have to disconnect, but it's a healthy choice."

I have no idea who she is referring to, but I can definitely relate to being on the receiving end of that disconnect. Healthy choice? Maybe, though I'm not sure for which party involved. I now realize pixies aren't meant to stay put ...they flitter through their world shining their light until they alone decide to flip the switch, leaving those they've touched in darkness. I've learned I really can't relate to pixies.

*Leah Vidal is the author of* Red Circle Days *and writer at* Little Miss Wordy. *Her writing covers a range of topics including current events, health and wellness, parenting and daily tribulations. While she enjoys writing about each of these, she is most at home when adding a personal element to a broad topic by sharing life's little moments...those that plant the thought provoking seed of self-discovery. She believes it is these moments that are life's biggest lessons. Leah is a 2014 BlogHer Voice Of The Year and her blog has been syndicated on* BlogHer, *featured on the* Erma Bombeck *site,* Freshly Pressed *on WordPress and highlighted on Fitness and Parenting sites. She has been featured on PubSlush Women Of Wednesday and is currently working on her second book.*

# AN EAR FOR LANGUAGE

LIZ DOLAN

The first time I realized Ag was crazy was at Walgreen's in the Port Authority. She had just returned from an 18 month stay in Berkeley, California, the haven of hashish, hippies and hedonism. Her yen to travel started after she had majored in French at City College.

"I answered an ad in the New York Times for a position as a nanny in Paris," Ag said, as she smoothed back her unruly red hair. "One odd thing, though, the father of the child requested a photo of me in a bathing suit, said we'd be spending lots of time at the beach."

"Sounds odd to me, too, Ag."

"But I need the job, great way to pay my expenses, practice my French."

"So get a job as a waitress; you'll cover your expenses, practice French that way. May even earn a few tips, but not the kind Frenchie wants to give."

Ignoring my advice, she worked as a nanny that summer in Paris, never mentioning the man for whom she worked again. In the ensuing summers she traversed the breadth of France absorbing the liberating influences of the Gauls. It seemed to me that she was shedding like a snake the repressive layers of the Bronx-Irish Catholic culture in which she had been raised. After ten years of teaching French culture and language in as many New York City public schools, Ag announced she was moving to Berkeley. For 18 months I never heard a word from her until a balmy September afternoon, "I'm home. It's good to hear your voice."

"I'm so busy reading all your letters, Ag; I hardly had time to answer the phone," I said as I washed the last dish in the warm, sudsy water.

"I'm sorry I never wrote."

"You're forgiven, but you' ll have to make it up to me by telling me all about the interesting men you met. You called at the right time. We're having a shower tonight for Rose at Diorio's on 45th street in Manhattan. The gang will be there. Come." Glad for a few moments alone after the shower, Ag and I stopped for a quick coffee in Walgreen's so we could really talk. She narrated a woeful tale of yet another unrequited love tryst with a guy, a much older artsy Irish immigrant whom she had followed to California, a detail she had neglected to mention to me before she left.

"He treated you like trash in the Bronx, Ag. Did you think California sunshine was going to improve his character?"

"I know, I know, but that schmuck is the least of my worries now. The FBI is after me."

"Why would the FBI be after you, of all people?"

"They're tapping my phone and reading my mail."

"Why are they after you?"

"Damn it, I don't know why. They just are. I'm afraid

they'll interfere with my getting another teaching job," she said, placing a napkin under her cup to absorb the coffee she was continually spilling because her hand was shaking.

"Please talk softly, Eileen. He might be listening to our conversation."

"Who?" I asked, glancing at the bearded drunk listing to the right on the stool at the end of the green formica counter.

"The waiter," she said. A short, skinny, pimpled-face 16-year-old refilled our coffee cups.

"Him?" I asked, laughing, my Sanka dribbling down my chin. Come on, Ag." Looking up at the octagonal clock smeared with grease, I realized I was going to miss the last bus home. Seeing that she was upset, I invited her to come for dinner on Saturday. I hugged her and told her she probably had jet lag. As I weaved my way through the homeless sleeping on the floors of the Hotel Port Authority, I wondered what the hell she had gotten involved in Berkeley. Riding up the escalator to my bus, I felt confident that the smog and traffic of New York would fix her up in no time.

Ag looked anything but upset when she arrived at my home, red-haired, relaxed, and radiant in red slacks and a red mohair sweater reminding me of Lucille Ball in "Auntie Mame." Ag looked as though she were reinventing herself. As I expected, she never mentioned the FBI but she did tell me she didn't think she could return to teaching.

"I was suspended before I went to California."

"Suspended! Why didn't you tell me then?" I stood by the sink with the kettle in my hand. "I thought we were best friends. For what?"

"Insubordination, absenteeism, lateness, no lesson plans."

"For God 's sake, Ag, those charges were easily documented."

"Easily documented, easily documented? Am I on trial here? The charges were trumped up by a black principal who was scoring points for himself. Of all people, you know I was a good teacher." Actually I didn't know if she had been a good teacher, even though we had taught in the same school together for a year, I had never been in her classroom, nor she in mine. "I'm sorry I bothered to come." She sat silent through the eye-round roast beef and mashed potatoes I had cooked for her. Sitting next to her at our pine dining room table, my husband and two little girls ate heartily but were baffled by her silence.

I begged her to stay over so I could drive her home in the morning. All night long I lay awake listening to her pacing back and forth downstairs in my white, beamed living room, the smell of her cigarettes wafting through the house as she chain-smoked her Marlboros. I felt ashamed that I was suddenly wary of her, but I kept getting out of bed, tiptoeing into the hall to check that the door to my four and five-year-old daughters' room was tightly shut. Totally surprised by what Ag had told me, I thought she had gotten caught up in the drug scene in Berkeley. Although I had always thought she was naïve, she had been a perfectly normal kid, at least to me. I remember the fun we had together when I used to go to her apartment for lunch.

Her tall, Olive Oyl mother, with her jet-black hair tied neatly in a bun at the nape of her neck, fussed about the yellow kitchen, the sun streaming through the dotted Swiss café curtains. "Eat more rice pudding, Eileen. Hurry up, Agnes. Stop picking the raisins out of the pudding! You're going to be late returning to school," her mother would say in a nasal tone that made me think her nose and mouth were inverted so she could avoid breathing the same air as the rest of us. I envisioned her words floating into, instead of out, of her mouth like little soldiers.

As we flew down the steps of 533, Ag pinged rice-coated raisins at me. When her wrinkled artillery ran out, she bounced her Spalding ball, crossing her leg over the pink sphere on every "A." "A, my name is Agnes and my boyfriend's name is Andy...," simultaneously dodging the cars on St. Ann's Avenue as we heard the cowbell signaling our tardiness. I sprinted up the street and attached myself to the fourth grade line, but I could still hear Agnes, mesmerized by the rhythm of her own voice, "E my name is Ellen and..." her leg turning over and over and over.

Years later Agnes' long leg almost got caught in the revolving door of Westchester Square Hospital, where we were visiting a close friend who had delivered a baby born with a cleft palate. "Your mom must have had a cleft palate," I said.

"A cleft palate? What's a cleft palate?" Ag asked, as we wended our way down the hall of the small marble-floored hospital.

"It's a separation in the hard palate on the roof of the mouth; it causes speech problems."

"Speech problems? My mother didn't have a speech problem!" Neighbors used to say an extra decade of the rosary after Mass on Sunday to avoid exiting the church at the same time as Ag's mother, rather than having to struggle to decipher her muffled syllables. How was it possible that Ag had never noticed it? I often thought her gift for foreign languages had developed from straining to understand the first voice she had ever heard.

Ag and I had played and had prayed together through eight years of grammar school. And on one particular occasion, we almost drowned together. It was one of those really hot days in early June when thirteen-year-olds are eager to cast off the restraints of the school year. A slight breeze rustled through the maple and sycamore trees which arched like a cathedral over Rocky Point in Pelham Bay Park, where we had decided to swim out to the moored sailboats and yachts, two lone swimmers in a prohibited area. Halfway to the boats, Ag suggested we should swim back to the shore.

"No way," I said. "The boats are closer. We've got to reach the boats." And so we floated, side by side, the ice blue sky ignoring our peril.

A red motorboat sped by. I waved and screamed, my voice drowned by the roar of the engine. "I can't keep floating, Eileen, I'm exhausted."

"Please, Ag. We're getting closer to the boats."

"Hail Mary, full of grace, the Lord is with thee," she prayed.

"Jesus, shut up, Ag."

"Pray for us sinners. Now and at the hour of our death, Amen." Even though I was ticked off at her for praying, maybe her prayers saved us. A boat finally rescued us. I will never forget the sound of Ag's voice praying that Hail Mary as I urged her to float on her back to save energy.

But in 1975, angry at both the FBI and me, she finally called me at 11 p.m. "I'm furious with my mother. She's forcing me to have a hysterectomy."

"Do you know what time it is, Ag?" I said, grabbing

my glasses to look at the time on the clock next to my bed. How could your mother force you to have a hysterectomy? You're 34 years old!" I said, as I sat up in my bed.

"Trust me, she'll find a way."

"Stop being so damned dramatic! Are you pregnant?"

"No, I'm not pregnant! You're supposed to be my friend; why are you always taking the other person's side?"

"I'm not taking anyone's side, but the whole thing is ridiculous. I know your mother. She would never do anything so cruel."

Five minutes later, Ag called again. "I think my mother is in cahoots with the FBI."

"Are you drinking? What the hell is going on? Do you know what time it is? My kids will be jumping up and down on my bed at six o'clock in the morning." Click, she hung up again. I lay in my bed with the phone cradled in my hand wondering if I was the one who was losing my mind, my husband next to me, still sound asleep.

A few weeks later, almost midnight, she called, waking me up again. "Somebody's breaking into my apartment. I'm afraid I'm going to be raped." Rape and burglary were not extraordinary occurrences in New York in the mid-seventies.

"Start screaming, Ag! Use the fire escape, call a neighbor, call 911!"

"It's my neighbor who's breaking in." I listened for noise; I heard nothing but the drone of Johnny Carson in the background.

"Calm down, Ag," I said, throwing off my down comforter and searching for the light switch. "Listen to me. You know I'm your friend, don't you?"

"Yes, I do."

"You know I care about you, don't you, Ag?"

"Yes, yes, I do."

"Then do exactly what I say: call 911 or a cab and go to the nearest emergency room. They'll help you. What hospital is closest to you?" I wished I wasn't so far away from her.

"Elmhurst General."

For weeks I could not contact her, nor anyone in her family. I finally received a letter which brought me enormous relief because I knew she was in safe hands.

*Dear Eileen,*

*Because I have been responding to treatment, the doctors say I will be able to go home soon. Unfortunately, my mother succeeded in her plan and now I will never have children.*

*Love, Ag*

Another letter arrived two weeks later.

*Dear Eileen,*

*I am happy to tell you that I will be released soon. In addition to getting an apartment near the hospital, I will also have an easy clerical job. My mother has had me lobotomized and mated with a bull. The FBI is reading my mail. Be careful what you write to me.*

*Love, Ag*

I asked my sister, a psychiatric nurse, if Ag will ever recover. "She's paranoid schizophrenic. Her best hope is thorazine."

"Doesn't it have horrible side effects?"

"Sure it does. Someday she may end curled up in a corner with her tongue flapping, but, at least she'll have periods without fear. Some schizophrenics see their own bodies attacking them. Don't be seeing her alone either. You two were always very competitive. She might be jealous of you."

Upon hearing of Ag's illness, a dear friend who had been our supervisor when we had been rookie teachers together told me she had recommended that Agnes should find a less stressful profession.

"She was my best friend and she never told me that. I was so upset when she left our school. Did you see signs of her illness back then?" I asked.

"No. I thought adolescents were too hard for her to handle."

And so she bounced from school to school in the big city system until she locked horns with a principal who had either the guts, the compassion, or the patience to complete the documentation needed to suspend a teacher. When I told my mother about Ag, she told me that Ag's mother was the only woman she had ever known in the old neighborhood who had had her husband arrested for abuse in the 1950s.

"It must have been a terrible situation that forced her mother to expose the privacy of her family in that way, the poor woman."

For 30 years I had considered Ag a close friend, but she had never really shared her deepest fears with me until there was little I could do to help her.

Today, instead of waxing poetic in her beloved French, Agnes babbles about Michael the Archangel and George the Dragon Slayer. Her babbling invades my dreams. Once again we are swimming, lost in the billows of the blue Aegean Sea. An Adonis stops his boat to rescue us just as the bronzed sailor saved us from the murky waters of Rocky Point so long ago. Rejecting the safety of Adonis' boat, Ag raises her right, then her left arm, in perfect arcs, pointing her fingers as though she is the star of a shimmering water ballet, her eyes glowing with serenity and wanderlust. "Give me your hand," I say, as I try to pull her into the silver boat. But it is as though the Sirens are luring her away from me and I have no wax to stuff her ears, to silence the voices that are pulling her farther and farther out to sea.

*Liz Dolan's poetry manuscript,* A Secret of Long Life, *nominated for the Robert McGovern Prize, will soon be published by Cave Moon Press. Her first poetry collection,* They Abide, *was published by March Street. A six-time Pushcart nominee and winner of Best of the Web, she was a finalist for Best of the Net 2014.She has received fellowships from the Delaware Division of the Arts, The Atlantic Center for the Arts and Martha's Vineyard. Liz serves on the poetry board of* Philadelphia Stories. *She is most grateful for her ten grandchildren who pepper her life.*

# THE FRIENDSHIP FAILURE

ARNEBYA HERNDON

I should have crossed the street as soon as I saw her. Common sense failed me that day. I was defiant, confident. Besides, what was she going to do? Attack me in the middle of the street? Turns out that, yes, that's exactly what she planned to do.

I quickly gave my friend, Melanie, who'd joined me shopping on our lunch break the run down: A few weeks ago I had not-so-nice words with a family member over the phone. She'd called me at an inopportune time. I was told to hang up. I hung up. And this family member was walking toward us.

My friend listened, horrified. I explained that nothing bad was going to happen and told her to calm down. It was the middle of the day, we were shopping, having Subway for lunch. Bad things don't happen to people eating Subway. Plus, I was planning a wedding, my hair was newly flat-ironed, and I was in a really cute coat. The odds were totally against anything bad happening.

Said the woman who just minutes later was involved in a physical fight in the middle of the street.

Oh, reader, don't make that face at me. We all have a minimum of one crazy-ass family member. Crazy covers all "special" relations: the druggie, the ex-con, the spoiled brat, the slut, the lush, the I'm-better-than-you-just-look-at-my-life person. And sometimes there's one person covering more than one type. I was dealing with a druggie ex-con. And I should have crossed the street.

I kept walking, though, determined to show her that I was perfectly willing to engage in a few eye rolls, lip smacks, and "Whatever, bitch"-es. Nothing else was going to happen.

In the end, the worst possible thing happened: Melanie let my sandwich roll into the drain.

The friendship was officially over.

In the early stages, our friendship was divine. We could talk about anything, and we did. There was no topic left uncovered. She was incredibly professional at work. It started to rub off on me, the girl who would call in more than once a week feigning a finely perfected fake cough. But then I started to notice that we rarely communicated outside of the workday. This was before texting took over actual conversations. I realized that all of our really good, informative, funny conversations never went into the weekend. Was this a true friendship if we never talked on a Saturday?

I tried not to pay attention to these thoughts. We were friends. We had lots in common. We were both engaged to be married. We were both in our late 20s. I was pregnant with my first child. And that's when the first inkling that maybe we weren't true friends after all was exposed. Another coworker confided to me that Melanie said my baby would be malnourished because I was too skinny to have a healthy baby. Melanie told me that she was misquoted. I believed her. She had great hair, and we were friends.

Two weeks later we found ourselves shopping at lunchtime, multiple bags in hand, facing an angry, druggie, ex-con cousin. And Melanie was about to show me that we were indeed not real friends. Don't get me wrong. I didn't expect her to fight for me or with me. But I also didn't expect for her to just stand on the curb with her eyes wide, not calling for help, not moving, not blinking, and not picking up my $5 foot long.

It happened quickly. We saw her approaching, and we went into Subway. When we came out, we didn't see her. But she was simply a bit ahead of us, behind a wall. She stepped out as we walked by.

She said, "The next time I call somewhere, bitch, you better not hang up."

*Be quiet, Arnebya, and keep walking.* That's what my mind said.

"The next time you call somewhere, don't say dumb shit" is what my mouth said.

And then she threw water in my face. I'll pause here to explain to you a bit about black woman culture. WE CANNOT GET A PRESS-N-CURL WET. My hair had been washed, blow-dried, and flat-ironed just days before. If it gets wet, it reverts to its natural curly state. While it's just as cute curly, half straight, half curled is not even half cute.

She threw the water, and then I threw a punch. She grabbed me and threw me onto the concrete easily. I weigh 108 pounds. She weighs 275. I just helped your visual. But, like most people tend to believe, she thought the skinny girl couldn't scrap. While I may not have been declared the winner, I got in a few good shots, namely one my sister taught me in seventh grade when I was about to fight a bully: kick her in the cooch. That 20-year-old advice came flooding back while I was on the ground, while she grabbed my hair and repeatedly slammed my head into the pavement. I kneed her in the stomach and then kicked her in the vagina with the square toe of my boot. She fell to the side with a yell that should have scared me. Instead it bolstered me. My newfound confidence was short-lived though, as she was quickly back on top of me.

I caught a glimpse of Melanie's face, and it enraged me further. She stood there, among a gathering crowd of people. People stood around watching, commenting, laughing. No one helped until we rolled into the street and a cab barely missed us. Its passenger jumped out, yelled to her to get off of me, that he was calling the police. And then it was over. With a final shove she got off of me and walked away, leaving me sitting between two poorly parallel parked cars. She never looked back, but I watched her walk until I couldn't see her anymore.

I did the walk of shame back to work alone, since Melanie had disappeared, with semi-curly hair, a dirty coat, no lunch, and no friend.

Melanie stopped speaking to me at work. She avoided me in the hall, stayed in the stall if I happened to enter the restroom while she was in there.

A few days passed. I sent an email asking if we could talk. Melanie couldn't believe my idiocy. What was wrong, she said, was that I endangered her life. What was wrong, she said, was I put her at risk. And no, we could not talk. There was nothing to say. We weren't friends. Whether she meant we never were or we weren't anymore, I didn't know.

A few years later I ran into Melanie and her husband, out with a group of people I was still semi-social with. Her husband spoke while she just half-smiled then looked away—you know, the stiff-lipped smile you give when someone says hello and you're too rude to say it back but you don't consider yourself rude because at least you smiled and nodded. Since then, I have replayed that day I was accosted, all of my conversations with Melanie, gifts we bought each other, to see how I missed the fact that we were never really friends.

I haven't seen her since then, but I wonder about her. Is she still married? Did they have more children? Is she enjoying motherhood? Does she have true friends? Our friendship may have been one-sided, but I was a good friend to her. I still think of her when I hear Prince's "Delirious." And I miss her conversation, even though I know I'm better off without her words or thoughts or opinions because we were never friends.

*Arnebya is the voice behind the lifestyle blog* What Now and Why, *where she discusses topics such as parenting, mental health, race relations, and healthy eating. A government contract writer/editor by day, Arnebya is also a married mom to three. A 2013* Listen To Your Mother *speaker and a three-time BlogHer* Voice of the Year, *Arnebya's writing has appeared on multiple online parenting sites. She is the recipient of a local DC award for fiction, the Larry Neal Writer's Award. Her work is also published in the* Washington City Paper's *fiction issue (2013). As a speaker at BlogHer's HealthMinder Day in 2013 on the topic of mental health in the online space,*

*Arnebya returns to BlogHer this year in the "writing lab" to discuss grammar.*

# ENCHAINED

---

MARY WANSER

We first meet when I am 10 and she is 31, the same age as my mother.

She seems to be at our house more than she is at her own, and I don't like it. Everything about her is too big—her presence, her mouth, her critique of the flaws on my preadolescent face.

She cans fruit in our kitchen. Her husband cheers at my sporting events. Her son, my peer, says he'll marry me someday.

I move out, I attend college, I move back in, and she is still around.

\*\*\*

"Mary Margaret will drive you home. Mary Margaret will take you shopping. Mary Margaret will help you with that." My parents find amusement in forcing a friendship they know I, now 20, don't want. Gradually, their efforts prove successful.

It was the language she used as mother that hooked

me—the pink Valentine's Day card she signed "to our daughter."

She helps me to wallpaper and paint my new apartment. She teaches me to thread a bobbin and sew. From her, I learn to roast a turkey, mash potatoes, and layer a cake.

There's something else she teaches me, when I've just turned 23 and she's not quite 45.

*** 

I am at home with a fever and cough. Her husband drives her to my house carrying a pot of chicken soup and he will pick her up again in a few hours. On the green floral bedspread with the lace border, she lies down beside me on top of the covers in her tight denim jeans. She rises up from my pillow, crosses one of her arms over the other to remove her T-shirt, and reaches behind her back to unclasp her bra. Her ample breasts fall to the side when she leans over to kiss me. My right hand cups her left nipple. I am scared and excited and confused and sick all at the same time. This is how it starts.

She dresses. Her husband honks. We say goodbye as if what happened never did.

After that first encounter, I rationalize. I'm her friend, her best friend. There is nothing I won't do for her. I was only helping to satisfy her curiosity. She knows I date men; she's met most of them.

I tell her by phone it will not happen again. I tell her we'll go to the library, borrow books on the subject, read them together, and she will learn. I tell her we will rent videos and watch them together so she can see. But I cannot be her study model. "Yes," she insists, "it will happen again." And she is right.

She swears I've done this before, and I swear I haven't. I hadn't.

I don't yet consider the incestuous undertones; I become her willing victim. Desperation devours integrity.

I don't remember her last safe touch, but each touch after that will be laden with shame and with guilt and with sin.

She tells me to flush my Prozac, so I do.

Her gay in-laws take us to underground establishments I didn't know existed outside of movies. Afternoon Tea at Lavender Hour was anything but that. Has she been here before? Do they know?

Years fold one into the other, and this becomes my life underneath my life.

I do things that readily perpetuate what I think is a love affair: I show up at her side door wearing nothing but a raincoat, I drive us to a toy store when she tells me what she wants and waits in the car, I make room for her clothes in my dresser.

"It's not natural," my grandmother says of my ongoing "friendship" with a married woman 21 years my senior. Grandma is more right than she realizes, yet the sordidness has become as natural to me as breathing. Me without her, her without me, that's where the wrongness is. But I can't explain this to my grandmother. Instead, I tell her I must return to work sooner than expected, that I must cut our visit short and leave her Florida apartment early. I hop a return flight back home to New York, back to the one I can't live with. Or without.

The ties become even more knotted when she starts calling me Mommy because hers has died. I am 30, and I like being needed.

She concocts other pet names for me—Mishka, Noreen, Marge. Some stick, some don't. I name a business of mine, years later, one she'll never see, *Mishka's Unique Boutique*. She names her new dog Mary Man.

Do I have an identity aside from her, I wonder? Gradually, I come to define my life and my worth by her.

I slip into a fantasy world where she is mine and I am hers. Together we pick out a pearl ring to fit my finger and a life-like baby doll that resembles me.

Christmas night and New Year's Eve become traditionally ours.

I long for a husband and children, a family of my own. But they are relegated to dreams in the midst of this nightmare.

I look to her for guidance. "What if someone asks? What am I supposed to say?"

She assures me, "People will believe whatever you tell them if you repeat it often enough. Deny it. Tell them they're crazier than hell!"

We steal each other from ourselves with a passion so possessive that we are hardly two people anymore. The only reminders of our separateness are the nights she spends with him.

The only things I do without her are in defiance. I take a vacation while she must stay home.

I can tell she is jealous. I intentionally display more excitement than I feel, I discuss my plans, I show her the brochure. With a sharp edge she asks, "What, are you planning to meet guys there?" "I might." And then I turn the knife. "Look, I'm not the one who's committed elsewhere, you are! I can go anywhere I want and meet anyone I want!" I hate saying it as much as she hates hearing it.

"Why do you want me? Because he can't get it up anymore?" I ask. She lunges at me, throws me down on their concrete driveway, and slaps my eyeglasses off my face, cracking them, and then refuses to have them repaired.

I draw two columns on a piece of scrap paper and make a list of why I should go and why I should stay. We discuss it in the same matter-of-fact manner we discuss what matching Halloween costumes we will wear this year. I stay put because we can't think of a believable enough response when people start asking, "What do you mean you aren't friends anymore?"

We fight and argue almost incessantly. She and I. I and me.

We drink, even from flasks on Sunday afternoons.

In her husband's presence, my stomach knots with the fear that we'll be found out, with the hate for him that masks my jealousy, and with the cordiality that covers it all.

There are questions that persist: What does he have that I don't? What makes him better than me, more protectable?

"Why don't we just tell him?" I ask her.

"Don't you dare!" she warns me. "He's done nothing wrong. He doesn't deserve to be hurt by this." I wonder why I do.

Our secret is hidden in the open. Our families accept us together. Her husband drives her to my office on Fridays so we can spend the weekend together, then I'll bring her back home on Sunday night. When he works the night shift, I stay at their home, in their bed, with her. Everyone knows we vacation together, just the two of us. They say nothing. And neither do we.

Her derogatory comments about my interactions with local high school dean who is older than she is, her utter disgust with interactions with him while still a teenager living in his basement, and her relentless insistence that I report to the district attorney all increase my shame and confusion.

"What makes this different?" I ask her.

"What?!" she shouts, rage in her tone.

I ask again, "What makes our relationship different from what I had with him?" I am desperate to know.

We are driving back to her house one Sunday night of many. I threaten to stop the car on the railroad tracks. And then I do it. She calls me a "crazy bitch" as the train approaches, and I don't budge the car. I can tell she is scared, so I pull forward past the gate. She doesn't get out; she knows I would choose her over me.

"Every time you go away, you take a piece of me with you," I tell her, my eyes wet and blurry. I won't see until years after we're finished that her being near is what was taking my life from me, not her ritual parting.

After eleven years of this, I exile myself from her. I know no other way to stop it than to flee to another state.

\*\*\*

On the day before I am set to leave, I find handwritten notes throughout my house—under my pillow, on top of the toilet, taped to the refrigerator door. They all say the same thing: "Don't go!"

I arrive in my new Florida home, open my suitcase, and there on top of my clothes is another handwritten note. "You should have stayed!"

A few weeks later, when I am still settling in, a

handwritten note arrives in the mail. "You better come home!" I don't. It's my self-inflicted punishment. And my saving grace.

He buys a fence to surround their brick house after I leave. It is composed of pickets, and it is painted white. I think it must have a gate that swings open because within five months she is visiting me.

Our days together are strained, but we are both crying as she boards the plane. I tell her, "Don't worry. You'll see me sooner than you think." I must have told her this before because when I get back home without her, there's a note on the kitchen table.

"Keep your promise. See me sooner than I think."

*\*\**

It takes me three years to build a business, buy a house, and make a life far away. Then I fly back to New York and call her from my hotel room. Before I can squeeze out the words, "Come home with me," she says, "I can't do that anymore."

I cry the type of tears that take the breath away. I wail and weep alone, in private. I wonder if she does too.

We manage to maintain the façade by phone calls and emails for nearly four more years. We try to carve out the rotten parts of our apple, but by then, there are too many worm holes and there's not enough nourishment to sustain us.

I can't remember how the pure parts ended, the friend and mother parts. I can't remember who said goodbye first. I just knew it was over the last time we spoke. Yet, it's still not over.

*\*\**

She stays with me like a film on my skin that won't come clean.

She once told me, "I feel sorry for anyone you'll end up dating because you'll always compare him to me." Again, she was right. There are invisible chains that enslave me to her. Distance and time do not weaken them, though she is another three years in my past.

I date men, but nothing lasts. I marry a woman who decides she doesn't want me either.

I'd been living with the secret for more than two decades.

As if with the same needle she had taught me to sew fabric, she stitched my lips closed, like a ragdoll who's not supposed to speak the secrets the little girl has whispered in her ear. Don't tell. Promise? But now, in one 50-minute session, one thread at a time, what she had weaved was unraveling. In bursts between sobs, I told the doctor what I had done.

My admission betrays her. My silence betrays me.

\*\*\*

The loss of her continues to grieve me. The fingerprint of her stains every part of my life.

I dream about her occasionally. Sometimes, she is loving me again, and, sometimes, I am angry. Always, there's a familiarity that won't leave me, even after I wake.

Sometimes, I wish I still had us minus the shameful parts. I miss her as my best friend. I miss her as my mother figure. I miss someone having my back. I still can't glance behind me and see her stabbing it, even though others can.

If I saw her today, would I run toward her or away? Both thoughts frighten me.

We have been estranged for five years, but our families are still very much entwined, into a third generation now. How do I lose the chains?

Inside of me somewhere, I think my surrender to her was done to spite my mother. She was her friend first, one who was willing to love me, albeit sordidly, when my mother could not. It's a knowing in a place deeper than I can reach right now, a truth I am not fully aware of yet, but somehow I know it's there. And I know that's not fair.

*Mary Wanser recently earned her master of fine arts degree in creative writing at the University of Tampa and completed her first collection of personal essays, a mosaic memoir entitled* Things I Wasn't Supposed to Say. *Her next project is pointing toward the self-help genre. A Long Island native, Mary now lives where two rivers meet in Bradenton, Florida as a freelance editor and private English tutor. She is an AWP member. You can find out more about Mary at* www.marywanser.com.

# WHAT WE DON'T SAY

ANDREA JARRELL

*Just we two,* my mother used to say. I seemed always to be re-creating the one-to-one closeness I had with her. Never more than with Liz.

We met on move-in day during our freshman year at a small college in Southern California—a gem of Spanish-style architecture with manicured lawns, hidden courtyards, and fountains. I was a local but Liz had come from Boston.

Later, she confessed that when I'd introduced myself her breath caught because she was sure I was about to say my name was Annabelle, a character in the Rona Jaffe novel *Class Reunion*, about lifelong friends who meet in college. She'd been obsessed with the novel all summer. Pulling the book from her shelf, she showed me the cover illustration, Annabelle with long red hair like mine. It seemed our destiny to become best friends.

Liz had grown up with a single mother, like I had, yet our maternal crucibles had made me one way and her another. I'd stayed childlike, naïve, forever pacing the sidelines of a grown-up world and wanting to jump in. Liz dove into the deep end on a regular basis.

On the first night of orientation, the guys from a neighboring dorm stormed our hallways, banging on doors and dragging girls from their rooms. I hid in my closet, convinced gang rapes were about to take place. After the whooping and shrieking died down, I emerged to find a group of flannel-nightgowned women peering into the courtyard below. On a makeshift stage, there was Liz in pajama top and panties linking arms with a row of girls doing a Rockettes kickline while 50 guys serenaded them. The next day, we admitted our shame to each other—me for hiding and her for giving them what they wanted.

Despite my lack of worldly ways, Liz was as drawn to me as I was to her. When I said I wanted to move to New York after college to become a magazine editor and write novels, she said, "Me, too!" She saw past the shyness others often mistook for conceit. In a college town full of Saabs and BMW's, I was hiding the fact that I was a scholarship kid. She was the only one I'd met whom I trusted enough to take home with me—to see how my mother and I lived. No doorman building or rose-lined front walk. Just a two-bedroom apartment with a carport in back.

Liz was fascinated by my mother—a woman on her own—who hadn't gone to college but had read every book on our floor-to-ceiling bookshelves and saved enough for us to travel through Europe by the time I'd graduated from high school.

She didn't judge me because I didn't summer on Martha's Vineyard like she did. Late at night in the dorm, she told me her Vineyard stories the way an exile might speak of her home country. Living alone with her mother, she felt the wrongness of her father's absence like the ache of a phantom limb. Only on the island was she whole again.

And when she ran across our dorm hallway wanting me to drive her to a pharmacy for the morning-after pill, I didn't judge her either. My virginity had become a burden I was all too ready to unload. "I don't want to shock you," she said after telling me she'd slept with the cute senior we'd met at a party the night before. She waited for him to call but he never did, the first of many men I saw take advantage of her.

After I met Liz's mother, I came to understand why she admired my mother's capability. Grace was in town one weekend to see Liz in a play. In slacks and turtleneck, she had the slim, athletic build of a tennis player and that old-fashioned upper-class accent you hear in Katherine Hepburn movies. She had the same big brown eyes and apple cheeks Liz had, but behind those eyes was someone playing along until she could get in on the joke.

She took us to a Mexican restaurant, where she ordered a Margarita with a lobotomized stare that made you want to snap your fingers in front of her face. I wondered if her blankness was why Liz's father—a civil rights lawyer—had left her. Or if his leaving was the cause.

Sophomore year, Liz fell deeply, almost violently, in love with our English professor. He was young, unmarried, and his classes filled up fast. He spotted her in the third row of Modern American Lit, and asked her to lunch one day when I wasn't in class. Not long after, he asked her to bed. As her best friend, I was in on their secret affair, which stretched into our semester abroad in

Paris, where he was on sabbatical, and continued once we returned to campus.

One day senior year, I ran into the professor. He was turning down the path to his house when he saw me. He asked if I'd take a couple of books to Liz. I stood just inside his open door as he rummaged around a dining table piled high with books and papers.

"Ah," he said, plucking the volumes from a stack. With his beaming smile, he walked toward me—books in his outstretched arm, shirtsleeves rolled, forearm flexing—and, as if it was the most natural thing in the world, kissed me. When I didn't kiss him back, he straightened and retreated to the dining room. For an instant I thought I'd imagined it. But as I met his eyes I knew he was already wondering if I would tell Liz.

I knew I never would. I couldn't risk our friendship by hurting her. Something else made me keep it secret too. Part of me had liked it. Not because I wanted him, but because he'd wanted me. It shamed me that a rivalry with Liz had begun to burn in me.

Oddly, people often remarked on our resemblance even though we looked nothing alike. She was tall and honey-skinned with delicate bones. I was fair, petite and athletic. But after years of being inseparable we just *were* alike. She stayed with my mother and me on weekends, celebrating Thanksgiving and Easter with us. I spent summers with her on the island doing all the things she'd told me about—beach bonfires, blueberry picking, milkshakes at the golf club. We started an alternative campus newspaper together and cohosted a radio show. We shared everything from sweaters to diaphragm jelly once I did lose my virginity. "Les Deux Femmes," people called us when we took a French class together. "Where's your other half?" they asked when one of us was spotted alone.

At first I liked it. Who wouldn't? Liz was smart and beautiful. But as we ran neck and neck, I wondered if I would be able to keep up and even if I could pull ahead.

As graduation neared, Liz spent most of her time at the professor's house. Then, without any help from me, she learned he was not to be trusted. She found his diary—a Pandora's box she couldn't resist. In explicit sexual detail, he'd chronicled encounters he'd had with her and another student on the same day. He referenced each girl by hair color—the sexy blond, the luscious brunette. I still wonder sometimes if he kissed me simply to add a redhead to his collection.

Liz and I did go off to New York to become magazine editors—or more accurately— lowly editorial assistants at competing women's magazines. We were grateful to land these coveted spots despite the paltry salaries. Liz's breakup with the professor had chastened her. No longer the girl on stage doing high kicks, she kept her head down and worked hard. I became more ballsy, dragging her to parties downtown, uptown, east side, west side, where we met SNL writers, bond traders, law students, and Julliard musicians.

It was the mid-80s—a time of blink-of-an-eye literary successes like Brett Easton Ellis and Jay McInerney. *Spy* and *Sassy* magazines were launched by young editors. I was 22. My boss was 25. People rose up the food chain fast. As I read through the slush pile and edited relationship columns, I no longer wondered if I would make it, I wondered when. Success seemed inevitable, like something you waited in line for until they called your name.

Then I got fired.

The editor-in-chief said, "In the future, you would do well to make your boss look good." Later, I learned the *Seventeen* editor I'd asked about a job had called my boss to report my disloyalty.

Like any good friend, Liz blamed my bosses, not me. But getting fired left me behind as she rose up the ranks, first at one magazine and then another. I found a new job soon enough, but without knowing it part of me had already begun looking for a face-saving exit from New York. A few months later, I found one in a guy named Wes.

I don't remember what Liz said when I told her I was moving to New Mexico with a handsome chef opening a restaurant in Santa Fe. I'd convinced myself I could live in an adobe house with him and write novels. I don't remember if she tried to stop me. Or if she, too, was ready for our paths to diverge. If I'd never gotten fired, I might still be in New York. Perhaps my friendship with Liz might even have turned out differently.

\*\*\*

"Where are all your clothes?" she asked, looking at the empty hangers in my closet when she came to visit me in Santa Fe. The trip had been a Christmas gift from her new boyfriend.

I didn't know where my clothes were. Maybe when we'd moved from house to house, a box of my jeans and t-shirts had fallen off the back of Wes's truck. Maybe I'd left the better stuff at a consignment store the way I'd pawned my jewelry. Like every part of my life—from my book collection to my limp, falling-out hair—my wardrobe had winnowed away since I left New York.

The truth is, the moment the plane touched down, I

knew I'd made a mistake. Wes wasn't a mean drunk like my father. He was a depressive one who spiraled into long, silent broods, lining empty wine bottles along the windowsills. When his restaurant failed, I'd gotten a clerical job. I'd written a few freelance articles for my editor friends back in New York, but I hadn't touched my novel.

"You've got to get out of here," Liz said as she looked into my empty closet. "Leave," she whispered when she hugged me goodbye at the airport.

It took seeing my life through her eyes to convince me. I went back to L.A. to start over. Driving over Mulholland on my way to a new job, I told myself I'd never lose control of my life again.

I'd been in L.A. for a couple of years the night Liz called to tell me her boyfriend had given her a ring. I returned her excited shrieks with my own as I thought *oh god, oh god, I'm being left behind.* The following summer, I watched her marry on the lawn of her grandmother's house on Martha's Vineyard. Her aunts teased me because I cried when I made my toast. Perhaps I didn't have the right to love her as much as I did or to be so proud. I wasn't family. But even as I worried I would never have what she had, her beauty and happiness pierced me in a way I would not feel again until years later when I had a daughter.

"I like the other one," she said to me on the phone a few months after her wedding. I'd been dating a lot of guys. At the moment, there was a lawyer and a Bank of America executive. But I'd also told her about someone I'd met while volunteering on a political campaign. We were just friends but he took my breath away. We'd been talking on the phone a lot, seeing movies together. Liz sensed from the start that he was the one. The summer after she married, I had a wedding of my own.

For a time after that, we seemed to be on the same path again. Like two sledders on a hill, she'd thrown her flexible flyer down, gliding smoothly on her way. I'd followed, flopping on my belly, unsure of the terrain. But now it seemed we'd reached the same destination. My detours and bad choices hadn't mattered after all.

Despite the adorable photo my wedding photographer took of Liz sitting in her husband's lap, her arms around his neck, I suppose there were some signs we were on different hilltops altogether. At the reception, I'd found her crying in the bathroom. She'd had the scared face of a child waking from a bad dream. She couldn't tell me what was wrong, only that she didn't want to go home to New York. "I'm okay. Don't worry," she kept saying, not wanting to spoil my day.

Not long after, she called to say she couldn't stop thinking about a writer friend of hers. "Maybe I should just sleep with him and get it over with," she said.

"There's no going back from that," I said.

Through the receiver, I heard her exhale. Then, "You're right," she said, as if I'd reached into the deep end and pulled her back to safety.

The year Liz had her first baby, I was in New York for a conference. Rather than a hotel, I'd been sleeping on her couch. Imposing on a couple with a newborn probably wasn't the best idea, but I was still operating the way we always had, taking any chance to be together.

We'd reserved the last day of my trip just for us—carving out the morning to replay our old days of scouring vintage shops and hanging out at the Columbus Bakery. What I wanted for our morning was a glorious fall day—the kind only New York City can unfurl before you. What we got was gray. What I wanted was our uncanny simpatico, each of us adding another building block to the conversation until it towered and toppled and we started a new one. Instead she stared straight ahead, gripping her wallet as if she'd just run out to buy a loaf of bread. In silence we walked down Broadway, her son in a Baby Bjorn like a star on her chest, his tiny arms and legs dangling.

In college, when Liz was overwhelmed by deadlines or heartbreak I would help her clean her room. Disaster made me want to scrub and vacuum. Not that day. Tempted as I was to wash her dishes, we'd left them dirty in the sink. We'd left hardwood floors in desperate need of a sweep. And we'd left her husband.

As rain began, we agreed to skip shopping and head to the bakery. Espresso machine hissing, muffins piled high in the case before us, we waited in line. Liz whispered, "I've got to nurse him again," and took off to find a table.

Trying not to slosh our coffees, I spotted her in a corner, Baby Bjorn unsnapped, shirt lifted. She watched me make my way. Did she feel the same rising panic I did? I tried not to meet her eyes, not wanting to say what was on our minds. For days, I'd pretended not to hear the yelling down the hall. I'd pretended not to be scared of her husband screaming at their crying baby, Liz screaming back. Their fights had been a train wreck out in the open, cars mangled, casualties moaning. I might have been the only one she would have let see them like that.

We both knew where talking about it could lead. The same way we'd known when she'd thought of cheating on him. Women alone raising children, what we'd both feared most. I remembered the apartment my mother and I first moved into. The way the lights went out when we couldn't pay the electric bill, the alley in back where I'd been molested after school. Always aware it was just we two, with no one else to help us.

I tried to concentrate on the cheeriness of the café. But Liz must have seen my judgment of her situation, my pity. Is that what made her reach for my wrist to check my watch? I had plenty of time before my flight, but she said, "I better get back. He'll be wondering where I am."

Out on the street, she stuck a hand in the air to hail a cab. A scrum of yellow taxis raced towards us, the victorious driver lurching to the curb. Liz cupped her baby's feet as she slid along the black vinyl seat after me. She called her address into the front. The cabbie tsked as he pulled away. It was the kind of short, low-fare trip cab drivers hate.

We'd barely come to a stop at her apartment when she stuck a twenty-dollar bill through the plastic window, saying, "You got the food. I'll pay for the cab." It was a point of pride. Her marriage may have been falling apart, but she could manage cab fare.

That's when the taxi driver said, "No."

"Excuse me?" Liz said.

"Need small," he grunted.

I reached into my purse. "It's okay. I've got it."

"No," she shushed me. "He can make change."

I caught the cabbie's eyes in the rearview mirror. He must have understood just enough to get the drift of our conversation, but he'd misinterpreted. He turned around in his seat, one arm hugging the wheel. "You play with me?" He glared. "Get out."

"Liz, I've got it," I said, but she didn't want my help. She shrugged at the driver as if to say, "Whatever, your loss." She put the twenty back in her wallet and we scooted across the seat, Liz cradling her son.

I thought the driver would peal off in a rage but he opened his door and climbed out. He was young and big. His short-sleeved shirt strained to contain his biceps and chest. "Stupid women," he said, towering over us.

"Here," I said, holding out money. Instead of taking it, he spit on the ground in disgust. Liz and I hurried up the front steps of her apartment building.

He followed.

She began to pat her pockets, and I knew she'd forgotten her keys. The cabbie stood behind us, shifting on the balls of his feet like a boxer. He puffed up his chest, directing his anger first at Liz, then at me. "I know where you live," he said.

Liz banged on the front door. We could see her building super through the glass. "Let us in," she called to him, but he didn't want to open the door because of the yelling driver. "Please," she said. "I've got my baby." Finally, the super opened the door. Liz slipped through, without even checking to see if I'd escaped.

Why I pressed my luck I'm not sure, but I turned to the cabbie and said, "We weren't playing with you." This time he drew back and spit directly in my face. "I know where you live," he said again. I reached for the closing door, feeling his spittle on the bridge of my nose and cheeks. Wiping my face with my sleeve, I saw Liz standing by the elevator, the button pushed. As we rode up, the driver's words lingered: *I know where you live*. But he had no idea. This was Liz's life and I was going home.

For years after the taxi incident, after Liz had another baby and I had two, I still called her my best friend. Even though it took her days to return my calls and sometimes she never did. Still, when I was in New York we'd get together, and on one of these trips she told me she was getting a divorce. She'd been dealing with it for over a year. It stunned me to realize I was the last to know.

What we didn't say, hadn't said, is that she'd divorced me long ago.

When I go to New York now, I don't call her, but I think of her every time. I think of a postcard she'd once tacked up in her dorm room: a couple on a bed with the caption, "This photograph is my proof. We were so happy. It did happen, she did love me."

Looking back, I think Liz stopped loving me on that rainy, gray afternoon we spent in the Columbus Bakery. Sitting across from me, stroking her baby's velvety head, scared about her marriage, she must have seen my relief. She must have seen the slightest glimmer of smugness I felt—how I was so glad to be me and not her.

*Andrea Jarrell's essays have appeared in* The New York Times; Narrative Magazine; Memoir Journal; Brain, Child; Literary Mama; The Washington Post; Washingtonian Magazine; Cleaver *and* The Christian Science Monitor. *She writes about love, sex, family, and mothering. She is at work on a collection of personal essays that build on her* New York Times *"Modern Love" column – "A Measure of Desire."*

# A 20 YEAR FRIENDSHIP GONE IN AN INSTANT

---

JULIE DENEEN

Some friendships die a slow death. I had a few of those. We grew apart or our children just stopped getting along. Once in a while a relocation forced us to part ways. But with Sarah, she was in my life one day, and gone the next.

I think death would have been easier than the passing of our friendship. She was a light in my life—a great bundle of energy and enthusiasm that never seemed to dwindle. I'd run to her house whenever I needed a cup of tea, a glass of wine, or a burst of inspiration. The 17-year age difference mattered very little, as our families bonded together through work, church, and social gatherings.

Sarah and I met when I was 13. She was 30. We went to the same church and she was the music director—I, the young whippersnapper piano player who didn't like to take direction. We weren't friends then, but our chemistry was unmistakable. By the time I got married nearly a decade later, we were close enough for her young children to act as flower girl and ring bearer in my wedding.

As the years went by, Sarah and I started playing music at restaurants together. We ran a Bible study and even merged our separate businesses into a partnership. Each and every year, we found ourselves more entwined in one another's lives.

But there were slow-growing issues within each of us, slow enough that neither one of us saw how they waited, like a ghost, to snatch our friendship's soul. Her marriage was in shambles. She tried to stay on the straight and narrow, but I watched as she slid into inappropriate relationships with other men while trying to keep her family intact.

Though I didn't have the same marital situation, I understood her guilt and pain. I too was in the midst of a very different sort of crisis. In February of 2011, I had an emotional reunion with my long-lost biological father, whom I hadn't known for my entire life, and that experience turned very dark. I suffered in a toxic and sexually abusive relationship with him for nearly a year before I got myself out of it. Sarah stood by me through it, as I stood by her crumbling marriage.

2012 was a year of healing. I gained national attention as I championed a cause for adult adoptees who were reuniting with their biological parents for the first time. I took all my energy and poured it into a mission I thought would make me better. But underneath, I was still deeply traumatized and questioning my faith and my identity. Since my relationship with my father was "consensual" (and I put that in quotes, because while he didn't chain me to a bed, I wonder how consensual things can ever be between a father and daughter...), a lot of people had difficulty understanding how a Christian girl could get swept up in something as twisted as incest.

2013 came along, and a lot of the initial media attention died down. I was unaware of how much healing I still had to do, and with that ignorance, came a grave mistake. I reconnected with my father in an attempt to quell the pain of continued abandonment and rejection. This sent my life into turmoil once more.

My husband Andrew and I separated in early summer because he couldn't handle watching his wife subject herself to such self-destructive actions. It was at this point that I even stopped reaching out to Sarah for help. I thought my life was too dark. Andrew and I kept our separation very hush-hush, not wanting to incite our conservative religious community to intervene, as we knew they would. My husband, having already endured this trauma once around, snapped himself. He took all his repressed anger towards me (and my father) and started making stupid decisions, and Sarah was in the line of fire.

She and Andrew always had a bit of chemistry, and whenever my insecurity about their relationship would pop up, Andrew would take care not to be alone with her or do anything that made me uncomfortable. But in the wake of this situation, those rules went out the window. We were separated and he was on a path of vengeance.

He began to pursue Sarah, and she had the initial reaction a good Christian girl would have. "Oh, but I can't," she said to Andrew. "What about Julie?" I knew that wouldn't last, for Sarah had a long history of doing whatever it took to get a man's attention. I knew their relationship was blossoming, but I didn't say anything. So deep in my own sickness with my father, I couldn't even muster up disagreement. In some ways, I was relieved.

Finally, I wasn't the only Christian person making terrible errors in judgment. And after all, my husband and I were separated. What could I do?

The helpless path I'd paved for myself lasted only a month, before I hit a suicidal low. At that point, I gathered strength I didn't know I had and broke off all the ties with my father. I started therapy and begged my counselor to give me the tools to free myself of him, and get my life back on track. I ignored my husband and my best friend, trying simply to focus on myself and my own healing. For a month, I let that relationship continue as I sought help. I even tried to keep my relationship with Sarah going—I was afraid that losing her, my husband, and my father would be too much for my grieving heart.

It didn't last long. Once I was free from my father's web, I ran out of patience for the rendezvous between Andrew and Sarah. I told Andrew it was time to make a choice. Try to work things out with me, or leave permanently. My heart was broken, but I couldn't imagine not giving him another chance after he'd stood by me through the ordeal with my father. I started to see that I had to fight for Andrew—I couldn't let Sarah take him away from me. When that realization hit me, all the anger that I wasn't previously able to direct at Sarah came rushing out in one of the most hateful emails I've ever written. I'm not proud of it, but I was also in the fight of my life. Between her friendship and my marriage, she didn't stand a chance.

Sarah never responded to my email. Andrew eventually agreed to break things off with her. We closed our doors to the outside world (the judgmental church community included), and focused on each other. I never heard from Sarah again.

Funny thing is, I still look back and think, "What if

I hadn't written that email? What if I had been able to forgive her for failing into the arms of her best friend's husband?" I still mourn her absence from my life, even after the betrayal. I miss Sarah. I miss the simple friendship that started those many years ago.

*Julie DeNeen is a full-time web designer and blogger, making her mark on the Internet with a tech blog called* Fabulous Blogging. *An award winning lifestyle blogger as well, she was chosen as Anderson Cooper's blogger of the day in 2012 and appeared on* Anderson Live *several times, as well as* BBC World Have Your Say. *Off the Internet, she is a mom of three, a musician, foodie, and theater buff.*

# GOING WITHOUT SUGAR

CHERYL SUCHORS

She hasn't died, but my best friend is gone.

We met when we were close to 30, friends of friends, at an outdoor concert called *SisterFire* near Washington, DC. On a grassy hillside surrounded by the sound of women singing rock and folk music, we talked. We were both single. She was a travel agent. I analyzed markets for a bank. We both were short, but where I was a line drawing, dark-haired and thin, she was a Reubens, full and fair. She had a way of touching your shoulder or arm as she listened and an intense, enveloping attention. Her touch was warm, gentle. She called to mind a phrase from Catechism classes in parochial school, "the laying on of hands."

Sometime later we had dinner at an Ethiopian restaurant, my first ever, in her funky Adams Morgan neighborhood. A bit high on honey wine, I said, "So. Tell me the story of your life." I was half-joking, but 40 minutes later, she was still talking and I was still listening. I remember we sat at a banquette, she looking out to the room, me watching her eyebrows soar. She filled my vision.

She began with childhood. Her family traveled and even lived abroad, making her exotic and worldly in my eyes. She didn't shy away from her parents' divorce, the family alcoholism (which I understood too well), her ravaged teenaged years. We had that in common, too.

"I can't believe I'm telling you this," she kept saying. I remember at first feeling embarrassed. It was so much more than I'd intended. Then I began to feel honored, beholden and, finally, close. It was as if I watched her life flow by in time-lapsed photography, as if I'd known her for years. I wished I'd tried this before when I met potential friends.

I admired the courage it took to reveal herself, and her sense of humor. She invented phrases I wanted to steal, a foreshadowing of how years later, I would answer my protesting daughter with her words, "Because I am The Evil One."

When she finished her story she looked at me. "Now you," she said.

I'd never auditioned for friendship like this, but I wanted to meet the standard she'd set. I ordered another glass of wine, then forgot to drink it while I offered her my childhood, as the only one in my family who didn't suffer from alcoholism or Down syndrome. I described our frequent moves, my four high schools, scholastic achievement as my salvation. I told more than I expected to, and found it liberating.

We began to loan each other science fiction novels and do laundry together on Sundays. We wandered the grounds of the National Zoo, always winding up at the white tiger and always talking. One night we went to a club and when no men asked, we danced by ourselves, imitating snooty punk rockers, sleepy hippies, disco queens. She made me laugh till I lost myself, a rare escape. Something in her healed something in me.

No one tells you friendship is a risky proposition, all the more dangerous for appearing so unfraught. We think it's utterly unlike romantic love. Though it's joyous to discover a new friend, even engrossing, we don't say we "fall" into friendship "blindly" or "madly," words that issue a warning. What my friend and I understood was that we built our friendship on shared values, occasion by occasion, and we believed that kept us safe.

After I moved to Boston for a job and married the man who followed me (and who's still my husband), my best friend and I stayed close through visits when we could, but mostly by telephone. "Hey, Sugar," she'd say, reminding me of the Southern mother whose passing I still mourned. "I'm running away from home. Wanna come?"

We tiptoed through our first long-distance fights, parsing them afterward until we each were okay. We grew secure enough to talk through jealousies, neediness, imagined insults. We always worked it out.

After she married, our families vacationed together, my daughter, four years older, pulling hers through the sea on a silver float. If I traveled, she kept my itinerary. "I like to know where you are," she said. I did the same for her. We discussed whether or not to color our graying hair and potential grade schools, high schools, then colleges for our daughters.

We chose to be best friends, beyond sisters, closer than blood. For decades, when something good or bad happened or I needed advice, I got to decide whom to call first: my husband or her.

I knew we'd be best friends for the rest of our lives—until her email, three years ago. *I'm really pissed at you. Please don't call me. I'll call you when I'm ready. I'm doing this to take care of myself.*

She'd just come home from a trip to her father's. He was ill and old and they weren't close. She said I wasn't supporting her enough.

Why not call and yell at me? We never fought by email. I was hurt, and scared. I also felt unjustly accused, angry. I fired back, *Well that's just ducky. Tell me when to call and what to say, so I'll be sure to please you.*

Afterward, I called to take back my snarky, unsympathetic words. I was also still mad. When she answered the phone, I asked what was going on and said avoiding me was infantile. As she had taught me so many years before, I insisted, "We need to have this fight."

She hung up. Another first.

When her father died soon afterward, we spoke. I sent her emails, cards. I called. We'd helped each other before through the deaths of parents and in-laws. We were my gold standard for dealing with hard times. But death roils emotional waters.

Another seismic email arrived. *Our relationship isn't working for me any more. I don't want to talk. I don't have the energy to process things, to work them out. I need, at least, a breather.*

What? When she had a problem, even her husband asked what I thought. Yet as her silence extended into weeks, I began to worry that somehow, beyond my stupid email, I had failed her.

I turned to other friends for help. "What did she say?"

they asked. "Did you make her angry?" At first I appreciated the opportunity to revisit each blow, hoping they could tell me how to bring my best friend back. Of course, despite their well-intentioned probing, they could not.

At some point, their stream of questions exhausted me. I felt as if I were going through a divorce and friends kept revisiting particulars, wanting to find reasons. They seemed to expect a hidden logic I couldn't provide, that might not even exist. Would they have kept asking "Why?" if I actually *had* been going through a divorce?

I wasn't divorcing, but we have no language for the collapse of a friendship. No civil or legal understanding exists to encircle, protect, or declare its existence. No public ceremonies seal the relationship or shore it up when rocks pierce the hull and we have to swim for shore, the sound of wreckage and cold seawater filling our ears.

*\*\*\**

For a year I waited. I wore the turquoise necklace that was her last birthday gift to me. The sofa became the sofa where she had held my hand as I stared at diagrams of my upcoming mastectomy and cried. With each mouthful of ice cream or chocolate or potato chips, I wondered if she were eating badly, too. My heart sped whenever the phone rang, but no one on the other end called me "Sugar."

Through it all, I longed for people to acknowledge the depth of my loss. To send a card, perhaps. To check in on me or invite me out to ease the loneliness. To honor the importance of a 27-year friendship and assume that I'd mourn when it appeared to be ending. Though we didn't have children or property together, we had our souls and our history and our expectations of the future to unwind.

Once, I called my best friend and got voicemail. She emailed back. *You are so brave. I wouldn't have the ovaries to call after a solid year.* But then nothing.

Months passed. I emailed that I'd fly to DC and see a therapist together. She emailed back she wasn't ready.

Then my daughter, a rising college senior, stood up for me. All on her own, she called the Auntie who'd loved her since birth. As they talked, my daughter said how much I missed my best friend and that I deserved, one way or the other, clarity. My friend listened, but made no promises.

My daughter's bold act honored the friendship in a way that helped me loosen the hold of my grief. When no decisive email followed her call, I was finally able to see how little of the friendship that had shaped my adulthood remained.

Slowly, I let go. I spent more time with the friends I had. Weeks went by where I didn't long for my best friend. My husband and I fulfilled our dream of hiking in New Zealand, and, for the first time, I gave my itinerary to someone else. As the waves of grief diminished, they left room for me to admit I wasn't sure I could trust her again. Even if she wanted to be friends now, it would be different. What we once were for each other had, cell by cell, collapsed.

When my birthday came around again, she emailed that we could talk about reconnecting. Before we could speak, however, a follow-up arrived. *I can't take this friendship back on.*

I won't say it didn't hurt. I will say I'm grateful. I finally accept that, like any other relationship, without two willing partners friendship cannot survive.

I wish I knew where to go to find a new best friend. I wish the world valued friendship enough that there were friendship rituals, like dates, in which both parties were actively looking. I wish someone would create a service that matched up potential best friends. I'd be the first to join. In the meantime, I am free.

*Cheryl Suchors' fiction, poetry and non-fiction have appeared in* The Distillery, Limestone, RE:AL, *and* Her Sports. *She's currently finishing a memoir entitled* 48 Mountains *in which, as a middle-aged woman and a cancer survivor, she hikes to reinvent herself. Cheryl blogs about hiking, writing and life at* Go For It . . . One Approach to Living.

# MOTHERHOOD

# THE BREAKUP

DOROTHY O'DONNELL

It wasn't as if I hadn't been dumped before. Or ended my share of relationships that had disaster written all over them. But this particular breakup hit me harder than most, even though, technically, I wasn't the one being dumped.

It happened at my eight-year-old's school on her first day of second grade, the hottest day of the summer. Seeking shade while I waited for the screech of the bell to release her, I headed for the courtyard with the big oak—the one the kids called The Barney Tree—by her classroom. The mother of Sadie's closest friend was already sitting on the wide, tile-studded concrete planter that surrounded Barney. I smiled and sat down beside her.

I liked Janet. I considered her my friend. We made small talk—about the weather, our husbands' annoying habits—as we had so many times before while we waited for our girls.

That summer, they'd spent hours bouncing on the

trampoline in my backyard, dissolving into peals of laughter as they played a game they called "Butt War." They dressed up like Hannah Montana and danced around my living room belting out "The Best of Both Worlds." They went to day camp together and called each other B.F.F.

Just before the bell rang, Janet turned to me and sighed. "I need to let you know what's been going on," she said.

My stomach clenched. I was pretty sure I knew what was coming.

She told me that during their last playdate, Sadie kept punching and pinching her daughter, Amy. It wasn't the first time this kind of thing had happened, she confided. Sadie had even kicked *her* in a fit of anger.

"I've never seen anything like it," she said, her eyes wide.

I stared at the tawny oak leaves scattered on the asphalt and pushed them around with my foot.

Sadie was diagnosed with early-onset bipolar disorder when she was five. Intense, sudden mood swings—including extreme irritability that can be triggered by something as innocent as a playmate saying "hi" to someone else—are symptoms of the illness.

Usually, she saves her explosions for home. It's where she feels safe to lose control. Maybe all the time she'd spent with Janet and Amy had made her comfortable enough to reveal her ugly side to them, too.

When the girls first became friends, I expected each playdate to be their last. Though she'd never physically attacked another child before, Sadie's explosions had pushed most of her few other companions away. But as the months rolled by and their get-togethers continued, I made myself believe everything was OK. I was desperate for my daughter to hold on to her one good friend. And Janet never mentioned any problems.

I'd told her about Sadie's condition, although I'm not sure if she understood it. And I get that. It's easy to see my little girl's outbursts of rage as bad behavior. Or the product of poor parenting.

I wouldn't want Sadie to play with someone who hurt her, either. But that knowledge didn't soften the blow when, as the classrooms' turquoise doors swung open and chattering kids flooded the courtyard, Janet said she thought our girls should "take a break." It wasn't hard to read between the lines: I knew their friendship was over. And so was ours.

I broke the news to Sadie as gently as possible on the drive home. She kicked the back of my seat and pummeled it with her fists. She shrieked that she hated Amy. But by the time I pulled into the driveway, she was sobbing as the realization of what her behavior had cost her began to sink in. Inside the house, she grabbed paper and crayons from a kitchen drawer to make a card.

"I'm so, so, so sorry!" she scrawled beside a giant purple heart with a sad face and a jagged line severing it in half.

I squeezed her tight and told her I was proud of her for taking responsibility for her actions. But I warned that the card wouldn't magically fix everything. She said she wanted to give it to Amy anyway.

I wish I could say that I handled the situation with as much grace. I didn't. I'd expected my child to be destroyed by the breakup. I wasn't prepared for how devastated it left me. I missed talking to Janet, who, like me, was an older mom with one child. I missed our occasional outings to the beach, barbeques and dinners at the girls' favorite pizza parlor.

Like a scorned lover, I obsessed over every conversation I'd had with my former fried trying to pinpoint the exact moment our relationship had soured. Was it the afternoon when she'd called me a soft touch when it came to discipline? Or the evening I showed up at her house to pick up Sadie and she'd hesitated a second too long before answering when I asked how the playdate had gone?

"Great!" she'd said with a strained smile, peering over my head into the dusk. "Everything went just great!"

The more I kept hitting the rewind button on our relationship, the more bitter I became. I went out of my way to avoid Janet at school. One day at pick-up time, I saw her walking toward me as I sat in the car line waiting for Sadie. She was holding hands with Amy and another girl I recognized—a docile creature, who, I was sure, never lost her temper or hit anyone. As I slouched in my car and watched the happy trio cross the parking lot, a wave of envy and anger crashed over me. How could they move on so easily with their lives after leaving such a gaping hole in ours?

I hit rock bottom a few weeks later. I was walking my dog in our neighborhood when a blue minivan chugged by. The driver lightly beeped the horn to say hello. I recognized the mother of the docile girl behind the wheel. I gripped Max's leash tighter, wondering if this woman lingered in Janet's living room to chat after playdates the way I once had.

From the back seat, Sadie's ex-bestie and her new sidekick turned to grin and wave at me. I feebly wagged a few fingers in return. What I really wanted to do was flip them off. Because I so wished that my daughter was crammed in the back of that van with them. I ached for her to have a normal childhood, for me to be a normal mom. As the van disappeared around a bend in the road, it felt like the life we were supposed to have was vanishing with it.

I yanked Max's leash and turned for home, ashamed of the jealousy and self-pity churning inside me. Janet had every right to protect her child. That's what mothers are supposed to do. It wasn't her fault that Sadie is the way she is. It wasn't my fault, either. A gray river of fog tumbled through the valley below the street where I was walking. I imagined it washing away the anger and pain I'd been lugging around since the break-up.

That night, I clicked on the website of a local support group for parents of kids with special needs. I'd thought many times about going to one of the group's monthly coffees but always found an excuse not to when the day came around.

The following Friday, I printed out directions to that morning's coffee and drove to the house. With a trembling hand, I pressed the doorbell. A woman with long black hair and a kind face opened the door and welcomed me. She led me into her living room where a dozen or so other women sat on a cream sofa and dining chairs, nibbling blueberry scones and talking. No one looked shocked when, after introducing myself, I told the story about Sadie hurting her playmate. They just nodded or flashed sympathetic smiles.

The next time I saw Janet heading across the school courtyard in my direction, I didn't look away. I said, "Hi," and asked how it was going as we passed each other. It still stung to know that she and Amy weren't part of our lives anymore. But I was finally ready to start moving on with mine.

*This essay was first published at Full Grown People.*

*Dorothy O'Donnell is a freelance writer who lives in the San Francisco Bay Area. She used to think training for marathons and triathlons was hard. Then she became a mom in her forties. Although she's written about travel, health and business, these days her main focus is writing essays and a memoir inspired by her toughest—and most rewarding—endurance event: raising a child with a mental illness. Dorothy's essays have been featured on* Brainchildmag.com, Fullgrownpeople.com, GreatSchools.org, Mothering.com, *and on NPR's Bay Area affiliate, KQED. She won a 2014 MAGGIE journalism award for her GreatSchool's story "Bipolar at 5?" Dorothy is a member of the Bay Area writing group, Write on Mamas, and has an essay in their first anthology,* Mamas Write: 29 Tales of Truth, Wit and Grit. *Visit her at dorothyodonnell.com.*

# TRYING

---

ELLINE LIPKIN

I once had a friend who, whenever she said the word "baby," had to knock three times on whatever was beneath her reach—a table, the ground, her bicycle—before the conversation could move along. I wondered about this quirk, but never said anything, wise enough to know, even at that time, there was so much I really didn't know about trying to conceive a child. Years later, when I started my own journey towards motherhood, I quickly learned never to underestimate the superstitions of a woman who wants to get pregnant. "Trying," I realized, when describing the experience of making a baby, is a word fraught with implications.

Almost always one to bump up against a deadline, the closer I edged towards 40 and the certainty that I wanted a child of my own, the more I found myself part of what seemed to be a fast-paced frenzy among friends who were all trying to squeeze in procreating after a rather peripatetic path through their 3os.

After we conceived just under the three-month

deadline my stern-lecturing doctor had given us before we were to seek help from specialists, my husband and I were thrilled. I found out I was pregnant on the morning we left for our belated honeymoon and for a brief period it felt like we were going to scoop all the golden eggs into our basket. After a teetotaling honeymoon with no raw cheeses or oysters, the bubble that the newly pregnant live within—a mix of excitement, fear, and anticipation when a second pink line finally tracks its way across a test—burst when I realized, at nine weeks, I was having a miscarriage.

And that's where the trouble started. After the pain (on all levels) wore off, I became what felt like a late-30s cliché of angst about waiting too long. I found myself increasingly becoming alienated from my group of friends who were also trying to get pregnant as I faced—grief-stricken, furious, and humbled—one of the first times I couldn't be successful at applying my best efforts to what I wanted to make happen. News of friends' need for maternity clothes, baby prep, and upcoming showers became hard to bear. My husband and I walked down a dark path with receding hope of what we'd find at the end of it, while everyone else seemed to be sashaying along, gleefully checking the developmental markers emailed from pregnancy sites each week. I realized that the initial thrill of being pregnant is an experience you get only once—as soon as something punctures the blithe expectations that project backwards from an estimated due date you never get that innocence back. The thought that friends didn't even realize how lucky they were, how smooth their path was, only infuriated me more.

This experience felt worse than being left behind when a friend got engaged, or married, or moved in with someone. It felt like treason, a betrayal that crossed each person over to the other side of a gulf that I just couldn't reach. I had never before realized how public getting pregnant (or rather, not getting pregnant) is, as I saw family and friends, upon meeting after a couple of weeks or months, surreptitiously sweep a glance towards my midsection. Unexpected embarrassment and a raw fury caused me to withdraw socially, as I sank deeper into a world of online fertility boards, with their alchemical mix of scientific treatments and old wives' tales, and a recasting of my future towards an image I had never imagined. The online community I found—women who were also bewildered, angry, and overwhelmed with sorrow as they struggled to understand the word "failure" and how it applied (to their bodies? to an IVF cycle? to their deepest aspirations?)—became the friends I could pull close around me. It was too painful to be near the friends who were physically proximate, but whose path veered so sharply from mine.

I had been close with my friend Rachel since our years in grad school. When she left New York for Texas for a new job, I mourned. When, a year later, I decided to accept a fellowship for (further) grad school in her city, she was the rock I clung to as I started my life over again. We were both thrilled to reconnect. Our romantic relationships waxed and waned, then waxed again, until a few years and a few out-of-state moves later, suddenly, we were both trying to get pregnant at the same time. We shared our initial hopes, what this would do to our still newish relationships, careers, and the different details she had to tend to doing this with her female partner. We helped each other parse what TTC, BD, AF, and BFP meant in the strange new land of trying-to-conceive websites (who knew?) and laughed at the absurdities of sites such as PeeOnAStick.com.

I could hear the hollow in her voice as she congratulated me on my initial announcement of pregnancy, and I knew how much this good news would hurt her. During the miscarriage that followed she was nothing but supportive. Just a few months later, when she announced her own first pregnancy, I was happy for her. But I also felt the same pang that sometimes caused me to cross the street when I saw a hugely pregnant woman approaching from down the block, so I wouldn't have to get too close to her fecund, blatant, unspoken, announcement. But at least I didn't feel rage, I thought, as I did towards a new member of my local infertility support group who got pregnant on her first round of IVF (first round!). When Rachel miscarried a few short weeks later, I knew I wasn't happy about it, but I had to admit I also felt relieved on some low, guilty level.

We were one for one (not that any one was counting) until I got pregnant and miscarried again. Then Rachel got pregnant again, and this one showed signs of sticking. As her pregnancy advanced, and I continued on what felt like a deepening path of frustration ("trying" taking on an even more desperate ring), I reached the point where I had to be honest with her—I emailed to say I just couldn't be in touch anymore. Her joyful news about her 20-week ultrasound and the excitement she felt was just too painful for me. As her due date finally approached, I ordered something off her Target registry and had it sent directly. I didn't call. I didn't email. I just couldn't do more.

My silence hurt us both. I *was* happy for her, but in my myopic despair I had begun to see the world divided into women who got pregnant (and stayed pregnant) easily and those—my group—who just didn't. Simply being around someone in the other camp felt impossible. After telling a co-worker the lengths I was going to in order to avoid an upcoming baby shower she said to me, "But you can't avoid your friends forever." "Actually, I think I can," was my response, although I wasn't sure this was such a good idea.

A therapist who had once visited my support group mentioned that the pain of infertility was something she believed no one else could understand except those who had gone through it—there was no comparable grief that even the most empathetic could grasp. That was how I felt at that time. The bond within my newfound community was intense. Monthly, we both cried and cheered each other on. There was no filter as we shorthanded our medical histories upon meeting with what felt like a secret handshake of acronyms (RE, FSH, IUI, IVF, the dreaded M/C and D&C).

When a member of this community met with "success" i.e. a pregnancy that lasted and, ultimately meant graduation out of the group, it was bittersweet. On the online community boards I frequented there were subgroups for women to express their feelings (guilt along with fearful relief) for, conversely, "betraying" their friends who were still struggling to have a child. Somehow, in this world, I could keep an even keel, mourning with others, feeling gladness at times. It was in the "real world," without the cover of anonymity, where it was too painful to see friends casually sail towards something I wanted so badly but just couldn't reach.

After two years of further isolation from friends who had crossed what seemed like an impassable chasm into another land, I was pregnant for the fourth time. It took until the 20-week ultrasound before I began to trust that I would end up with a baby in another 20 weeks. When my husband and I left the appointment, I said to him, "After all we've been through, we need to start enjoying this," although I was well aware that for those in my camp, who were used to skating the thin edge of doom, a kind of PTSD worry never really leaves you. But I realized I wanted to reach out to friends and to share this news and I could no longer keep hiding my pregnancy at work, ironically enough, at a feminist magazine.

When I cautiously reached out to Rachel to let her know I wanted to be in touch again, she was nothing but gracious. She welcomed me back and we were able to pick up where we left off. I wanted to hear about her labor and delivery, what those first few days, weeks, and months at home with her baby had been like and to feel her warmth again. Her good will towards me hadn't left, but had gone into storage. I felt grateful beyond belief, especially that she understood why I had to pull away.

A couple of years later, when I was deep in the throes of new parenthood (sleepless, distracted, and cranky), and living in Los Angeles, I started fielding calls from Alex, a friend who had moved across the country to follow her boyfriend. I knew her deepest wish was to have a child, and she wanted me to know they were, at long last, ready to "try." When they finally conceived, and she then had her first miscarriage, I offered all my empathy. When they conceived again, I found myself deeply bound up in the drama of whether or not this pregnancy would hold.

I suggested she not get her hopes up too high, and remember that while a positive pregnancy test was a fine start, there was no reason to believe that there would be a baby at the other end of nine months—the way I had come, through necessity, to pragmatically view this process. I felt her get testy. "I only want positivity around me now!" she practically shouted into the phone, "only positive energy!" I knew how fragile, on all levels, that initial period of pregnancy is—and I knew she was entitled to her hope. I didn't want it to be taken away from her—and I didn't want to be the one to crack even a hairline of doubt into it. I hadn't meant to be hurtful, but the cloud of her anxiety in those uncertain first weeks reawakened my own vulnerabilities. After a few more brief emails that communicated good results, I checked her Facebook page after not hearing from her for awhile. I was shocked to see that I had been unfriended.

I reached out over email to ask why, and Alex said she felt, while pregnant, too anxious to communicate with me. My warnings hadn't gone over well. I was truly stunned. I wrote back to say that I hoped she knew I was offering this as a way to ward off what I viewed as the greater hurt—especially after her first pregnancy didn't hold.

I was also hurt by the feeling that I was tainted because of my past experiences, and this was the reason she wanted to distance herself, an unexpected ripple of isolation still reverberating years down the line. But I knew I had to let this—and to let her—go. The memory of my own recurring disappointments had crossed a wire, and I was trying to protect her in a way she didn't need or want. I also remembered how, in that period, no one could say anything helpful to me—not the "it will all work out" well-wishers, not the doomsday-sayers who casually offered up their horror stories, not the "why don't you just adopt" suggestions from those who knew nothing about what this really entailed, not the cut-and-dried "these are the stats" medical professionals, not the "believe and it shall be" acupuncturist I visited—just no one.

In those blurry first few weeks, after landing on the "other side" into new motherland, even taking the baby out on a walk, his tiny toes peeking out from the side of my Ergo as he nestled against my chest, made me wonder who I might be hurting by just carrying him. Sensing glances from other women passing by, I knew somewhere among them there was one who had cried in the bathroom last month when the tiny white pregnancy test screen came up blank. There was surely at least another one or two or three who was trying mightily not to sob while attending a baby shower, and who might, in fact, now be crossing the street just to avoid passing me.

*Elline Lipkin is an academic, poet, and nonfiction writer who has also worked as an editor for a variety of publications. Chosen by Eavan Boland, her first book,* The Errant Thread, *won the Kore Press First Book Award and was published in 2006. Her second book,* Girls' Studies, *was published by Seal Press in 2009. Endorsed by Peggy Orenstein,* Girls' Studies *explores contemporary girlhood in the United States and how gender is imprinted from birth forward. Currently a Research Scholar with the Center for Study of Women at UCLA, Lipkin teaches poetry for Writing Workshops Los Angeles as well as private workshops. Her nonfiction writing has appeared on Salon.com and she is widely published as a poet. She writes a book review column, "Off the Shelf" for Girl w/Pen: Bridging Feminist Research and Popular Reality.*

# DIMINISHED RETURNS

---

ALEXANDRA ROSAS

The number one reason people leave a relationship is something called diminished returns: you don't get back what you put in. Your effort does not equal your expected results. This sounds like an easy enough formula, but what if your expected results are never expressed? If you don't ask for what you want, are you right to feel wounded when it doesn't come your way?

Female friendships are complicated. Women are social creatures bound by our biological nature, by the need for others to help us gather food, watch our children, and help us after birthing. We haven't changed much in the thousands of years we've walked this planet; we still seek out the shelter of others to make our way lighter.

My husband and I moved away from a large city when we started our family. We wanted the opposite of what we each had growing up. When we attended a small town's strawberry festival, we knew it was where we wanted to live. Within the year, with our first child barely two and a newborn, we were moved in. The jarring shift in environment from city to small town made me feel as if tumbleweeds were blowing past my window.

With two babies and my new stay-at-home mom status, the loneliness was relentless. I was exhausted because of the move and the lack of sleep, but with the first spring day, we were out for a walk. I needed to find a clan who would help me with the weight of my new roles, being home and being a mother. The isolation I now felt had stripped me of everything I thought I was, and my quiet, introverted life was gone forever. As we approached a park, I saw a gathering of women and small children. My hands grew sweaty at the thought of saying hello to strangers, but I needed someone to talk with. I pushed the double stroller up to the park ahead, and hoped the moms there would not be a clique, their friendships already set in stone. As we got closer, I could see the tall willows, swings, and four picnic tables with tablecloths. Gripping the stroller's handles, I rehearsed the way I'd introduce myself. Would my face show that I had been without a friend since I had left my job?

Heading toward the tables, I saw a beautiful woman, not in appearance but in spirit, standing in front of the group. Her voice was loud, but what she was saying was drowned out by laughter. She wasn't shy, telling a story with arms animatedly flying over her head and wide-open-mouth gusto. In the middle of her sentence, she turned her face to me, and with the kindest smile I had seen since winter, she said, "Good Morning! Hello! I hope that you and your beautiful children came to join us! If you didn't, then now you'll have to! Come over here. You don't have to stand alone over there…"

And like water to a thirsty man, I took her in. Could she be a friend? Would she be *my* friend? She obviously had a legion of followers, but could I hope to occupy a small corner in her life? She finished what she was saying to the group, and everyone moved on to playing in the sandbox or giving out snacks to their toddlers. She walked over and, making a spot on the bench, she introduced herself.

I quickly told her about the boys and about how being a mother and not working and living in a small town with a husband who traveled was getting to be hard. I didn't expect to, but my eyes welled with tears. "Oh, honey," she put her arms around me and held me in a way that only made the floodgates open. "Here," she told me, "this is my phone number. We meet here in the park every Wednesday, but I want you to bring your boys to my house—we have a huge yard and I'll invite some other moms. We'll have a picnic! Everyone! Come say hello to Alexandra and her beautiful boys!"

It wasn't until the boys became antsy after three hours in the park that I reluctantly packed everyone up and said my good-byes. I had talked to people, I had an invitation, I might have a friend. I waited until the next week to call her and I left a message. I didn't receive a call back, but I knew I'd find her at the park for the Wednesday morning group. At ten a.m., just like the week before, she was there. Again, at the center, with another charming story. She greeted me with another enveloping hug and I told her I had called and left a message. "I'm so sorry, I'm really bad at phone calls. How about you just drop by? Here's my address. I'm always at home and I mean it, drop by." After a few hours at the park, we headed back home, but it felt so good to be with people.

Early the next week, I was driving home from the grocery store with the boys. I knew her home was out of the way from my house but I decided to go past it anyway. I wouldn't knock on the door, but if she was out, I would tell her I was just stopping by. Her home was obvious to me before I knew where it was—her children were playing in the front and she was on a lawn chair, her phone up to her ear. She saw me drive up and motioned for me to join her, all the while maintaining her phone conversation. I laughed when her youngest said, "My mom has phone messages to return! You have to play and be quiet!" She had instructed them well. We stayed for ten minutes, and then I moved to leave. She covered the mouthpiece, "No! Stay! Just give me a few minutes." I sat back on the grass and we played a bit longer. As it approached lunch time, I knew I'd have to leave soon. I told her I'd be back another day, not so close to lunch. "Good! I'm so happy you came by! We'll see you at the park!"

On Wednesday morning, we were back at the park, and so was she. Surrounded by five women, she was telling them of something so good, no one could tear themselves away. I stayed on the fringe, pushing my children on the swings. When it was snack time, I walked over to say hello. She gave me a beaming smile and told me she was so happy I stopped over to visit earlier that week.

As spring grew into summer, and summer into fall, I'd see her at the park. Without fail, she welcomed me with smiles and hugs. I would leave her messages to have dinner or a quick lunch at my house, inviting her to bring her children. She never returned my calls or mentioned them to me at play group. I'd drive by to visit her, and she'd make me feel that she was happy to see me, though she was never without the phone to her ear.

Then the winter came, and the playgroup at the park vanished. There was an indoor moms' group at our local church, but without play equipment my children would grow restless and we'd have to leave early. I was beginning to feel cut off from the world again, and so one morning, I called her. This phone call was different from the rest. I told her I needed her to call me back, and that I really needed to talk to a friend

A few days went by and I still hadn't heard from her. On the fifth day, I left a message, "Please call me back. I really don't know anyone and I'm having a hard time. Do you have just an hour? Could you visit? Please bring the kids." Nothing back, though I had seen her on the phone plenty of times.

One morning it was warm enough for a winter walk. I tucked a blanket in around the boys and we headed for our small downtown area. My heart sank when I walked past a coffee shop window and saw her inside, laughing with a group of women. The rest of the day, I struggled. Old feelings came back of being rejected, of not being enough for someone to want my friendship in return. These were all my issues, not hers, but the brief glimpse of her that day knocked those feelings out of the closet I had managed to push them into.

When we were back home, I called again. "Hey, just checking in, I saw you out this morning and it looked like fun. Call me, let me know if you'd ever like to get together. It's Alexandra." I made it sound casual, but the heaviness in my heart felt anything but that.

The years went by, summer always coming back, and I would see her at the park. We knew each other now, but our relationship never went past a hello and a hug. It had never become what I had hoped it could. After being a mother of two for six years, I was joyfully pregnant again. I called her with the good news, "Call me!" I said.

Again, no call back. But at the park and when I'd see her in our small town, she eagerly greeted me with laughter and smiles.

Toward the middle of my pregnancy, I entered pre-term labor. I was put to bed rest and had a long five months in front of me. This was winter, how would I survive the solitude of being alone and not being able to leave my house? I called her, "Could you please call me back. I'm high risk for early delivery, and I could really use a visit." I waited for her to call back, hoping I'd have company. Nothing back again.

I cried into the side of the sofa while my children napped. It wasn't so much about her as it was all the negative self-talk that flooded my mind. It was about me, why was I not worth a friendship to her?

We made it almost to full-term with our third boy. He was born a month early and spent a week in NICU. I called to tell her that our son had arrived, but that we wouldn't be coming home right away. I asked her to call back, I needed a pep talk. She never called the hospital.

I've made friends since we first moved here, and though we're busy with our lives, we send an email or a text to say we're thinking about each other. Most importantly, I have found a life online, too, which has made it easier to stay in touch when you only have minutes here and there throughout your day for a quick hello. I've found my tribe, my writing tribe, and I have people in my life now who understand me in a way I've always wished for.

In retrospect, I see that I hung on too long to this hoped-for friendship because of my loneliness. There were diminished returns from the start, but my need for the friendship was also great. I can't put the blame on her. I had never told her what I hoped for. I'm the one who accepted the no calls back, without setting an expectation. I wanted more than she had room in her life to give.

I could argue that she should have returned my calls, but, truthfully, she didn't have to. Did she do anything wrong or say anything wrong? Was there ever a dispute or disagreement? Did she betray a confidence? Was she dishonest or deceptive or did we drift apart? Was there anything wrong with me or what I did? If you had asked me any of these questions 15 years ago, I would have given you a different answer. But today, the answer to all these questions is no.

I recently saw her on a crowded Saturday afternoon at the grocery store. She gave me a warm hug and told me how big her children are getting. She asked me how I was and I told her it was a tough year—I had lost my nephew and my mother. She gave me another hug and told me to keep in touch and we said our good-byes. As my cart turned the corner, I heard her greet someone else excitedly.

I pushed my cart down the aisle, trying to go back to my list, but my eyes were too blurry with tears. I thought about how I had lost a friend, but she had merely lost an acquaintance.

*Alexandra is a first-generation American who writes humor and cultural memoir for several websites. She was* BlogHer Voice of the Year *in 2011, 2012, and 2013 and was named a* Babble *top 100 Mom Blogger. Alexandra proudly presents with the award winning national live storytellers tour* TheMoth.

# BEING THERE

SUZANNE BARSTON

I sit in my bathroom, hands pressed to my face, pushing into my temples as if the pressure could hold back the thoughts. I don't know why I get so angry, or why the anger turns inward, causing me to rake my jagged nails over my body, punishment for its audacity not to conform to the standards I've set for it.

There's a knock on the door. "Suz?" The door opens, just a crack, so I can see the edge of her face, the shape of one almond eye.

"Yeah," I mutter, not wanting her to come in, knowing that she will. She always pushes her way in. That was how we met, years ago, the first day of freshman year. She wouldn't take no for an answer then, and she won't take it now. I know this, just as I know she likes ham slices topped with strawberry jam, or how her face turns bright red when she's drunk.

She enters, sits next to me on the tile floor. I avoid her eyes by focusing on her feet. Her polish is chipped on one toe, and our grout needs cleaning.

"Do you want to talk about it?" she asks.

I don't, but I do. She understands this. She puts her arm around me, talks in low tones, makes me put words to the thoughts in my head. It's a delicate dance, but she knows the steps, and after six years of living together she does them seamlessly. Thirty minutes later I am in the kitchen, eating food that she's made me, warm pasta and overly-garlicked vegetables. Eventually, I feel better. Calm. Known.

***

I've been let down by nearly every close friendship I've had. Female friends were too mercurial, too confusing with their shifting affections, petty jealousies, social strategies. Male friends wanted too much of me, and then not enough. I don't trust easily. But I trusted her. It took a few weeks, sure, but once she had snuck her way into my heart with her southern accent and complete disregard for social cues (I don't know how many times I shut my dorm room door in her face, thinking I wanted privacy or space, when it turned out what I wanted was her and her bag of potato chips, spilling crumbs all over my bed while we watched The X-Files), I accepted her as something different. A sister. A soul mate. We'd joke that we were each other's first marriage; that any man who came after would be a distant second.

Even when she moved to New York, and I stayed in Chicago; even when her career took off and mine stalled out; even when she made bad choices or I made bad choices, we remained us. When the planes hit the twin towers, she was a few yards away. I was miles away, on the phone with her, screaming at her to get underground, gripping my television screen as if I could teleport her to my safe apartment in an untouched city. Twelve years later, when people ask the inevitable "where were you when," I struggle to answer, because I felt like I was there. My heart was there. My better half. I *was* there.

***

That same year—the one that everyone associates with grief and fear, change and evolution—I met my future husband. The week before our wedding, he and I got into a horrible, clichéd fight. She was the first person I phoned, hysterical, wanting to call off the wedding. She was there, pulling me off the bathroom floor once again, guiding me to reason, leading me back from the edge.

I said my vows. And she was there, next to me, crying sappy tears, giving sloppy emotional speeches. She was there, in another bathroom, fixing my poorly-altered wedding dress with safety pins.

My husband and I moved to Los Angeles, and she was still there, visiting as much as her schedule allowed, calling me daily to report on the soap opera of her love life.

***

I had a son. And she was there, but something had shifted. I found myself in another bathroom, hating my body once again for not conforming—not being able to nourish my child the way I was supposed to, not able to stave off the dark cloud of postpartum depression. But this time, it was my husband who forced his way in. She was still there, on the phone, but distant. This time, she took no for an answer. She didn't demand I put words to my thoughts. So I didn't.

My son grew, and she was sort of there, sending gifts for his first birthday, checking in by phone periodically, but never digging deeper, assuming I was blissfully happy, because why wouldn't I be? I was a mother and a wife.

She was the one with a career and drama and illicit affairs with coworkers. There was no space in this narrative for my ambivalence towards motherhood, my secret, hot jealousy of her freedom and success, or her many friendships and frequent travel. There was no room in the script for her silent longing for security and partnership. So we said our lines, convincingly, and our scenes grew shorter and shorter.

I became pregnant once again, but she wasn't really there. She found out over Facebook.

I had my daughter. She was there, once, stopping by on a work trip. We pretended nothing had changed. It was artificial and awkward; a bad sitcom where the actors had forgotten how to play their roles. Maybe we didn't know what those roles were, anymore, lost as they were in assumptions and resentment and sadness.

She got married.

I wasn't there.

My marriage began to fall apart.

She wasn't there.

I don't know who left whom, or if anyone really left at all, or rather just failed to appear. There was no fight, no deep, irreparable hurt. But it's more painful, that way. It's a slow bleed, an internal injury. You don't know you're in trouble until it's too late.

*** 

I sit in my bathroom, hiding from my children, not wanting them to see their mom in tears. It's scary seeing your mom cry. I know this, like I know how my son still makes appreciative noises when he eats something delicious, or how my daughter likes to fall asleep stroking the side of my face.

I would call someone, but I don't know who. My

friends now are all moms, all in happy marriages, content with their lives. They only know me as a mother. They don't know my darkness, the demons that plagued me through my teens and twenties. They don't know how to anchor me. How could they, when they only swim in lakes, and I'm drowning in an ocean?

I want her. I stare at my phone, scroll down my contacts list. I pause a moment, realizing I don't even know if she still uses the same phone number.

I call. But she isn't there. She isn't ever there.

There's a knock on the door. "Mom?"

The door cracks open, and I see one almond eye. My son's.

I pick myself up off the tile. I go and make my children dinner; hot pasta and overly-garlicked vegetables.

And eventually, I feel better.

Calm.

But never quite as known.

*Suzanne Barston is the author of* Bottled Up: How the Way We Feed Babies Has Come to Define Motherhood, and Why It Shouldn't (*University of California Press, 2012*), *and a freelance journalist whose work has been featured in* New York Times, the Huffington Post, SheKnows.com, Mommyish.com, Kids In The House, Pregnancy & Newborn Magazine, Parenting, Babytalk, OhBaby!, *and many more publications and websites. Suzanne Barston was honored to be one of the keynote Voices of the Year in 2012 for the annual BlogHer conference. A graduate of Northwestern University, she is currently at work on her first novel and runs a women's writing collective in the Los Angeles area.*

# LOSING CHLOE, LOSING JEN

---

JENNIFER SIMON

It was a wedding that cemented our friendship and a wedding that proved our friendship was over.

Chloe was friends with my friend Amy, and although we had met a few times, we didn't get to know each other until Amy asked us to go away with her for a bachelorette weekend. Before you get the wrong idea, it was not the typical sorority-style bachelorette nonsense. There was no champagne or clubbing involved. Instead, seven of us rented a van and drove from New York City to the Catskills for a weekend of thrift shop searching, white-water tubing, BBQ eating, bad movie watching, trashy magazine reading, and cheap vodka drinking. It was glorious. Merely acquaintances when the weekend started, by the end, we were inseparable.

If ours was a romantic relationship, that was the weekend we would have told people we had fallen in love.

Like me, she was self-deprecating, funny, and sarcastic. Single, we both dated because it was fun, not because we were necessarily looking for boyfriends. We both took advantage of living in and exploring New York City. At the time, many of my friends were either party friends who I texted after 10 pm or daytime friends with whom I met for brunch or shopping. But Chloe was the rare, all-around kind of friend. A real friend. She was just as fun getting a few drinks as she was the next day, getting pizza in the Lower East Side. Ours was a whirlwind courtship—within weeks we were professing our love for each other.

We had a great time drinking and dancing and drinking some more at Amy's wedding. While there, I met the last in a string of inappropriate guys I would date for a few weeks. Pretty soon after, I started dating Matt, the man I would marry. As soon as I met him, I knew he wasn't boyfriend material; he was husband material. Kind, generous, gainfully employed and, like me, Jewish. It was as if I had ordered him! Like a good friend, Chloe wasn't disappointed she has lost her cruising buddy; instead, she was happy for me.

She liked Matt and welcomed him into our circle. At the time, Chloe was dating a guy the rest of us liked too; however, much like her previous boyfriends, he was an underemployed musician/wanna-be filmmaker with a drinking problem. Chloe wanted to get married by that point, but after several years of dealing with her boyfriend's inability to commit (plus his blackouts), they broke up. Right after their breakup, I got engaged.

Once again, Chloe was happy for me. We squealed over rings together, debated the playlist, and marveled at all the nonsense that went into planning a wedding. If I had had wedding attendants other than just my sister, she would have been one of them. Instead, she handed out programs and then danced all night to celebrate with me.

What do women do when they get married at 31 and don't particularly like their career? They get pregnant. And I did, a few months after getting married. Chloe was delighted and declared herself an aunt-to-be. And I was delighted that she had started dating Luke. I didn't know him very well, but the few times we hung out, he seemed like a good, decent, interesting guy. And, most importantly, he seemed to have a mellowing affect on Chloe.

I have never been an all-or-nothing person. I'm more wish-washy, willing to linger in a state of gray instead of making a commitment. Because of this, I tend to gravitate to charismatic, intense people like Chloe. Definitely an all-or-nothing kind of person, she was Type-A, passionate, and dedicated to whatever her goal was at the time. Over the course of our friendship, she evolved from a hard-drinking, crap-eating, guy-cruising, financial analyst to a Kombucha-brewing, vegan-cooking, health counselor and Pilates instructor. I liked both versions of Chloe. Although one of them was into junk food and one-night-stands and one of them was into kale and exercising, she was still pretty much the same person.

But new-and-improved Chloe didn't know if she was ready to settle for Luke. He was too fat. He didn't work out enough. He didn't eat healthy enough. He didn't challenge her enough. I married my "Nice Guy," and I was hoping Chloe would realize that "Nice Guys" don't come around a lot and that a relationship with Luke was worth cultivating.

We discussed our nice guys while she trained me at Pilates and we met for lunches. After all, I couldn't get drinks or go out much anymore. We weren't in our twenties, drinking our nights away—we were in our 30s now, looking ahead to what our lives were going to be. And my life had turned into the timeline Chloe wanted. My husband was a lawyer. I did freelance PR and writing work. And I luxuriated in my pregnancy.

As a modern, feminist woman, however, I was extremely cognizant of what I did not want to happen when I had a child. I was determined not to sacrifice my own identity for the sake of my child. Motherhood would not define me. I would remain "Jen" instead of becoming "Mommy." I would not forget to carve out "me" time, and I would remember that if I didn't care for myself, I couldn't properly care for my child. I would make time to see my friends and not assume the world revolved around my baby. Unfortunately, like many great plans, mine were not to be.

I delivered Noah via emergency c-section at 2:03 am on a Tuesday morning in November. It was a harrowing, scary experience, but once we knew everyone was safe, I was in awe over how much love I felt for my scrawny, purple 4.5-pound baby. Two days later, Chloe and a mutual friend came to visit us. She cooed at my tiny baby and joked about how much he looked like Matt. I didn't learn until later that she had broken up with Luke that very morning. She was ready to get married but didn't think he was ready to commit.

After getting home with Noah, I, like many new mothers, felt overwhelmed, insecure and out of control. But for the first couple of months, things were manageable. He nursed, I rocked him to sleep, he woke up, he nursed, I rocked him to sleep. Rinse. Repeat. He woke up a lot at night, but he was a newborn. I was full of new-mom hormones and love and adoration. But after a couple of months, his sleeping habits were no longer normal. He was crying every hour at night and was waking up for the day at 4 am. Every day. Cute baby love wasn't cutting it anymore. No advice books—not even a sleep consultant—could help him sleep later.

Regardless of how cognizant I was about not losing myself and not letting my child consume my life, it happened. Everything I swore I wouldn't do, I did. My worst fears came true. I sank into a black hole of motherhood and for months and months and months, it felt like there was no way out.

To say the times were bad is an insult to bad times. My latent anxiety disorder blossomed into full-fledged, crippling anxiety. It manifested itself physically, climbing up my arms and spider-webbing across my back. And, while I was sure I was doing a terrible job at mothering, I also felt like I couldn't ever leave Noah. Even leaving him with Matt while I walked to the corner to get my nails done (an ostensibly nice break) nearly gave me a panic attack—I felt as if a physical part of me was missing. When I had to leave him the first time to attend a wedding, I called his sitters (my friends) no less than 13 times in the three hours I forced myself to stay out. I was a neurotic mess.

I spiraled into depression. It seemed like things would never change. It seemed like nothing would ever get better. That the daily fights Matt and I had were tearing us apart. That my son would never, ever learn to sleep like a normal person and I would never sleep again. I cried everywhere I went—at his pediatrician's office, at our Mommy and Me class, at the grocery store, on our walks. It got to the point where I was afraid to leave my apartment, not fearing where I might start crying, but that I might never stop.

Finally, finally, I got the help and medication to function, but by then, there were deep rifts in all my relationships. After all, it seemed to many people, especially Chloe, that I had abandoned them in favor of a new, "perfect" life. Whenever I tried to tell her things were less than stellar, or in fact, awful, she didn't understand. How could she, really? How could anyone who hasn't experienced it understand the particular torture of sleep deprivation?

To the outside world, I had it all: a husband with a good job and a beautiful baby. But the truth was that I didn't want any of it. Yes, I was lucky enough to be able to stay home (at that point I had stopped freelancing), but it was less a choice and more a result of the crippling anxiety I felt when I had to leave my son and the depression that prevented me from functioning like an adult, let alone working in a professional environment. And yes, I was married, but it was a hollow, deeply damaged marriage. Some days I could barely bring myself to look at my husband; often, I was mean and hostile toward him.

Although it seemed like nothing could go right in my world, in Chloe's world, things were changing for the better. Shortly after they broke up, Luke told Chloe he was ready to commit not only to her, but to her lifestyle. So, while I spent 18 months in a perpetual fog of anger, depression, anxiety, and sleeplessness, they spent it exercising and exploring the Brooklyn vegan foodie scene, as well as doing all the normal things couples do like seeing movies, grabbing a beer or just going out to dinner. Things that had become as foreign and unattainable to me as sleeping past 4 am.

It was no wonder I drifted from all of my pre-baby friends.

By the time she got engaged, we really weren't hanging out anymore. Then again, I didn't hang out much with anyone, especially someone who didn't have a screaming kid at home. But I was happy for her. I still cared deeply about her, and I was thrilled to go to her engagement party. I got dressed! I left the kid at home! I acted like a normal human being! I brought a small gift, had a half of a beer, and got to be "Jen" for a bit instead of just "Mommy," just like I had planned almost two years earlier. Chloe told us the wedding would be over the summer and I promised we would leave Noah with my in-laws for our first weekend away from him.

A couple months later, I realized that if she was having a summer wedding, she would have already sent out a save-the-date card or email. Which I had never received. I checked with Amy and sure enough, she had sent a mass email providing details about the wedding and the heads-up on the invitation to come.

I told myself that I understood why I wasn't invited. After all, we weren't nearly as close as we had once been. And even though nothing really had happened to cause our "breakup," we were in different places and it was natural for friends to drift apart. I made peace with it.

And then a few months later, it happened.

It was a Thursday. Like every Tuesday and Thursday at noon, I picked Noah up from preschool. Like every Tuesday and Thursday at approximately 12:10, I walked into my building and checked the mailbox.

It was one of those moments in your life that seem to happen in slow motion.

First, I saw a longer, fancier envelope than normal—one shaped like an invitation. Next, I saw the return name—Chloe's name. I was overwhelmed with relief and happiness. Like somehow the invitation was a bridge, spanning the tenuous, difficult last two years and connecting our previous friendship to a current friendship. It was literally an invitation to maintain or even restart our friendship. *I'm invited to her wedding! Of course I'm invited to her wedding; I was invited to her engagement party. Of course I'm invited to her wedding; we're still friends*, I thought, joyously. Stupidly.

Because that's when I noticed that the name on the envelope wasn't mine.

I fought against the inevitable tears. It was hard not to take it as an insult. A personal affront. She had sent me an invitation to her wedding. Only, it wasn't for me.

I swallowed. The rush of anger and sadness and humiliation made me feel sick. I knew instantly what must have happened: I was on the 'B' list and she had addressed the letter to another friend with a similar last name but used my address instead. So now, not only was I not invited to my former good friend's wedding, but I had been sent an invitation to her wedding meant for someone else.

Once I got into the apartment, I called Matt shaking, crying. *Maybe it was for us*, he tried to assure me, *and she just wrote the wrong name by mistake.* My mom said, *Maybe if it wasn't for you, she'll do the right thing and tell you that it is. Maybe she'll invite you anyway.* I knew they were wrong.

Collecting myself—deep breaths, deep breaths—I was determined to be the bigger person. So, after I calmed down, I left her a message saying that I had gotten the invitation addressed to someone with a similar name and asked if she would like me to send it back to her or throw it away. I wished her well. I hung up. And I tried to go on with my afternoon.

It revolved, like every afternoon since I had him, around Noah. I made him lunch. I got him ready for a nap. After his nap, we painted. We listened to music. I made him dinner. All the while, I was thinking about the invitation.

Until I got that envelope, I hadn't admitted to myself how much I actually wanted to go to Chloe's wedding. Yes, I thought it would be a fun party, but more importantly, I wanted to remember what it felt like to be myself again. I wanted to experience the kind of life that I had abruptly left two years earlier.

She returned my call at the time of night when everything collides into a mess—that time when whatever calm previously existed is replaced by the rush, rush appointment hour of bedtime. And the phone rang at the apex of that time—teeth brushing. Although Noah was too young to need to brush his teeth, at least with fluoride, we still went through the routine each night to get into the habit.

The phone rang. I answered it.

"Thanks for calling. I appreciate you being so mature and adult about this," she said, letting me know immediately that yes, she had made a mistake and no, she was not going to invite me anyway.

After the initial adrenaline spike from hearing her voice again, I fought to remain calm. "Sure, well, I only want the best for you," I replied, squirting the BPA-free, dye-free, fluoride-free, non-GMO, organic, BPA-free, obligatory Brooklyn-mom toothpaste onto my son's toothbrush.

We talked briefly before I had to go—I didn't have time catch up with my old friend about her new life—my obligations were to toothbrushes, pajamas, and bedtime stories.

As I hung up the phone, I was overcome by sadness. Not just about losing my friend, but also about losing myself. When I started crying, Noah hugged me. I tried to remember who I was before I was Mommy, when I was Chloe's friend, when I was Jen. And I held him tighter.

*Jennifer Simon is a former Kansan who clicked her heels landed in NYC over 13 years ago. A freelance writer, she blogs at The* Huffington Post *and has contributed to* Scary Mommy, Mommyish, Women's Health Online, Kveller, The Frisky, *and* Nerve. *Jen lives in Brooklyn with her sons, a baby and a sleep-challenged 4 year old. A former publicist, artist and fun person, she is now a very tired lady. You can follow her on Twitter at NoSleepInBklyn.*

# FROM HAPPY HOUR TO HAPPY MEAL

SUE FAGALDE LICK

Maddie was matron of honor at my wedding. We were so close I couldn't imagine anyone else doing that job. But I haven't seen her or spoken to her in over 20 years. I don't even know where she lives.

What happened? Babies.

Back in my newspaper days, Maddie sat at the next desk. We chased deadlines and wrote headlines together. Although she was married and I was divorced, we went out, we spent time at each other's homes, and we confided our deepest secrets to each other. We looked so much alike people thought we were sisters. It felt like it.

Things changed sometime between the day I matched her glass for glass when she had to chug water in preparation for her sonogram and the day she stopped eavesdropping on my phone calls at work and started talking to the baby in her womb.

By the time her son was born, I was still talking news, but for Maddie, it was babies, babies, babies. She quit her job to take care of little Sammy, but we tried to stay in touch. Now instead of meeting for drinks, we met at playgrounds, amusement parks, or McDonald's.

It kind of worked. We were still friends when I met and married Fred. But it all went to smash when Maddie's second son, Jason, was born. Not a sentence went by that wasn't interrupted by either Sammy — "Nobody's listening to me! I want to talk!"—or Jason, who couldn't talk yet, but wailed like a broken smoke alarm.

A single thought could take an hour to communicate. Our worlds had become so different. I had not had any children with my first husband, and now I never would. Fred, 15 years older than we were, already had three children from his first marriage. He did not want to have any more kids, and his vasectomy assured there would be no "accidents." The fact that I had always wanted to be a mother was irrelevant. My life still revolved around work. But Maddie and I tried to keep up our friendship.

***

One memorable day, we decided to go to Happy Hollow, a children's park and baby zoo in San Jose. Our first stop was lunch. Maddie and her kids had arrived so late the morning was gone and we were all starving.

"Look at me. Did you really expect me to be early?" Maddie asked, brushing greasy hair out of her face as she struggled to unhook Sammy's seat belt while Jason whined to be nursed. We chose fast food.

I guess you get used to being embarrassed. The waitress kept scratching out the orders and starting over as Maddie tried to get across in sign language that what she was saying to placate her son—"I want a large soda!!!!"—and what she really wanted—a small soda—were two different things. The line grew behind us as we went through the entire menu one item at a time. "Would you like a hamburger?"

"No!"

"A chicken sandwich?"

"No!"

"Chips?"

"No!"

Ah, just get him a prefab kids' meal and move on, I thought.

When we finally settled at a table, Jason reached for Maddie's sandwich, and they both wound up with tartar sauce all over them. Meanwhile Sammy was finger painting the orange plastic table with ketchup.

Maddie decided Jason needed to nurse. She lifted up her tee shirt and unfettered a milk-swollen breast. She claimed nothing would show, but I could see it plainly, and surely the man just coming in the door could see it, too.

My cheeseburger was long gone when Maddie passed Jason to me and went for another fish sandwich. "I eat so much when I'm nursing," she explained. Then of course Sammy wanted another sandwich, too. She promised him an ICEE when we got to the children's zoo. That ICEE was held up as the bribe for every good thing and punishment for every bad thing he did throughout the afternoon. "Help me with this seat belt and you'll get an ICEE." "You don't get an ICEE because you didn't help." "Mom, I tried." "Well, okay, you can have an ICEE."

At the zoo parking lot, it was time to change Jason's diaper and nurse him again, the breast coming out as Maddie sat on the curb rocking the baby. It must be true that new moms become unaware of everything but their babies. I would never get the chance to find out.

Meanwhile, Maddie failed to notice that Sammy was pushing the empty stroller into the path of every car that came along because he thought it would be cool if it got run over. I finally grabbed the stroller, wondering how she managed both children when no one else was around.

Sated, Jason rode quietly in his stroller, playing with the colorful little toys hooked on it, but Maddie warned me it wouldn't last, and it didn't.

We stopped at a puppet show. Eight zillion kids, all under age five, none of them really interested in the show. The performance was mediocre, the plot thin, and the puppeteers kept holding up signs—"Yay, boo, hiss"—ignoring the fact that the preschool audience couldn't read.

Five minutes into the show, Sammy needed his third bathroom stop in less than half an hour. Then he wanted to climb in the nearby tree house. Jason whimpered in his chair, pawing at my shirt. Nothing there, kid.

Behind me a little girl coughed, her cherry ICEE-stained tongue sticking out. In front, a family noisily divided a cluster of grape popsicles. All around me, moms and toddlers fidgeted and hollered. Nobody was watching the show. Except me, the one without a kid.

After the puppet show, Sammy went down a caterpillar-shaped slide backwards and intimidated a little girl into following suit. She crashed and ran sobbing into her mother's lap. Later when Sammy cut in front of another girl, Maddie yelled that girls always go first. To me, she added, "Might as well teach him that shit now." What happened to feminism and raising our sons to respect us as equals?

Finally, having heard about it all afternoon, we hit the snack bar for the ICEE. Of course the next stop was the zoo, where a big sign warned that food and drink were not allowed. We disobeyed the sign, and Sammy dripped cherry syrup all over the railings as he watched the animals.

By now, Jason had become a siren, screaming with his blue eyes wide open, his hands clenched and his feet up near his face. "Do you hear anything?" Maddie asked, determined to ignore him.

Well yes, as a matter of fact, I was losing years of hearing by the minute.

We had barely entered the zoo when Maddie stopped to nurse Jason again in front of the brown bear. Sammy scampered to the wallaby cage. He stuck his hand through the bars and gently pet one of them, talking softly and sweetly to his new friend. The sign said, "Please keep your hands outside the cage." Luckily, Sammy and the wallaby were just the right size for each other and neither was damaged.

The wallaby hopped toward its food dish, its oversized testicles dangling between its rear legs.

"What's that hanging down?" Sammy asked.

Oh God, I thought. Am I supposed to teach him about the birds and the bees and the wallabies? "Well, it's a boy wallaby."

"Oh, is that his penis?"

Close enough. "Yeah."

I looked around for Maddie. She was holding Jason up, rubbing noses and whispering in his ear. As Sammy stopped to slurp his ICEE, scooping out bits of red ice with a long plastic spoon, I went ahead to the next cage alone and struck up a conversation with a raccoon. He seemed to understand my frustration.

Visiting the zoo isn't the same for a four-year-old as it

is for an adult. Grownups walk in an orderly progression from exhibit to exhibit, reading the signs and admiring the animals. Kids wander aimlessly, more interested in the ICEE they're dribbling down their chin or the crow eating popcorn on the path than all the wild animals we keep pointing out. They're too short to see over the fences and bars anyway. And when they see the gift shop, it's all over.

His mother tried to distract him. "Look Sammy, look at that bobcat over there. Isn't he pretty?"

But it didn't work. "Mom, can you buy me that?"

"What, dear?"

"That stuffed animal."

"No, Sammy."

"But I want it."

"I said no."

Suddenly the goats that ate out of his hand, the giant pig and the hamsters under the parrot perch were of no interest.

"Look Sammy," I tried. "Look at the raccoon. Isn't he cute?"

"I don't care. Mom, why won't you buy me anything?"

"Because you don't need any more toys. Let's go look at the giant tortoise."

"Who cares? I want to go home."

He wasn't the only one. As we approached the exit, Maddie ran back to the refreshment stand for frozen grape juice, because she was thirsty and Sammy refused to share his ICEE. I held Jason, wearily pointing out the sights—the now-closed ticket booth, the duck pond full of leaves and pollen, his brother jumping into a rental stroller and riding it around like a souped-up tricycle.

Maddie returned and Sammy added a tinge of purple to

his cherry mustache as Jason started to cry again. I guess what they say about babies and cars is right. He was asleep by the time we finished the two-mile trip to my place, his sunburned cheek resting on the side of his car seat.

"Well, I'll bet you won't go out with us again," Maddie said, putting her hand over Sammy's mouth as he started to speak.

"Oh, don't be silly. I had fun," I assured her. We set a date for the next month at a historical park, where I would spend all my time taking pictures and talking to myself.

***

Our friendship ended the last time I went to Maddie's house for lunch. She had moved from San Francisco to the suburbs in the East Bay. When I arrived, she was babysitting another child in addition to her own. She'd forgotten I was coming, but assured me she'd get the kids taken care of and we'd have a nice meal. But she never found a minute for me. For two hours, I sat looking out at her spacious back yard and chatting with the parakeet chirping in its cage in the living room while she comforted wailing toddlers, struggled to make child-friendly lunches for them, talked on the phone and called out now and then that she was sorry but she'd get to my lunch soon. Eventually, my blood sugar crashing and seeing no end to the mom business, I told her I'd come back another time. But I never did.

No one said anything, but it was clear there was no room for me in this relationship. If I had had children, too, I suspect everything might have been different. Maybe, like Maddie, I would have retired to fulltime motherhood, and we would have shared our children's experiences from birth through high school and beyond.

But we lived in two different worlds, and our friendship died as a result. I changed jobs, we both moved, and we lost track of each other.

Most of my friends these days don't have any children around. Either they never had kids or their kids grew up and moved away, so they have time to do things without them. Not always. If their children or grandchildren need them, they're gone. I'm sure I'd be the same way. But I don't have children, only dogs.

Maddie's children must be adults by now. She might have time for me, or we might find we no longer speak the same language. I'll never know.

*Sue Fagalde Lick is a writer, musician and dog mom. Author of* Childless by Marriage *and* Stories Grandma Never Told, *she lives near Newport, Oregon with her canine best friend Annie. Visit her website at* http://www.suelick.com.

# GIRLS, INTERRUPTED

---

ALEXIS CALABRESE

The first time I heard Pachelbel's "Canon," I was a sophomore in college, sitting on a cold dorm room floor, wrapped in a Mexican blanket. My roommate Erika was playing the cello alongside her friend on violin. They started slowly, coaxing music into the chilled air with their bows, while I sat stunned, letting my Camel Light burn down to my fingertips. The solitude of the piece brought tears to my eyes and when they finished, Erika laughed, dismissing it as fluff.

"Wedding fluff!" she spat, as if nothing could be worse. Erika was like that, unaware of her impact, content to let others take the spotlight while she clapped from the sidelines. We were part of a tight knit group back then, a motley crew really, but it was Erika's cool and cultured bohemian streak that struck just the right balance with my uptight nature. She was the wild flower to my potted plant. She let things slide while I held on to every last shred, clinging and obsessive.

"Just shrug it off," was her advice after a minor breakup

with a very minor guy. "Don't let this dude hang out in your kitchen." And by "kitchen," she meant my head. She was right. There was no point in agonizing over it, dissecting every moment with tweezers, as was my habit. It was over. I took her advice. I learned to shrug.

After graduation, Erika and I always circled back to each other, traversing years of slave-labor jobs, crummy apartments, boys, men, and then marriage and kids. She wore my veil at her wedding. I was one of the first calls she made when her daughter was born.

"Look at my person!" she exclaimed when I met baby Ella for the first time. "She's perfect," I said, looking down at her navy eyes.

Erika was warming a bottle next to a pile of dirty dishes. Clothes littered the floor along with boxes of wipes and mail that had been knocked from the counter. She floated around the chaos, immune, while I fought every instinct to not grab the vacuum. Her smile was the calm in the storm.

My son Jay was born the following year and at nine months old, just when I started getting the hang of the Diaper Genie and burp-free bottles, he was diagnosed with a mild form of cerebral palsy. He had survived an in-utero stroke, leaving him partially paralyzed on his right side. The symptoms were only just beginning to show and our world started crumbling down around us. Erika was one of the few people who stuck around to watch the dust settle. Turns out, talking about a kid with a serious medical condition can kill a friendship faster than saying "I have sister wives."

"We have to start OT and PT right away," I said, choked with tears after an initial hospital visit.

"I don't know what that means," Erika whispered.

"Me neither," my voice cracked with the realization of how far from normal my life was becoming. I had gained access to the club that no parent wants to be a part of, the missing chapter from the *What to Expect* book. It was the saddest time of my life, and yet, one of the most clarifying.

Soon after Jay was diagnosed, my husband Charlie and I made the tough decision to sell our house and move to a different state to access better schools and therapy programs. We sought out the best doctors, learning as we went, forging through toddlerhood then preschool. Rather than succumb to the crash of that wave, we swam against it, with everything we had.

I started to meet other parents whose kids had special needs, our own distinct language setting us apart on the playgrounds. I met Lydia, a blonde beauty with biceps like Madonna, whose nine-year-old son was about to undergo a hemisphrectomy, a procedure where surgeons remove part of the brain to help alleviate seizures.

"Tons of yoga and really good red wine," was the answer she gave me after I asked how she kept it together. Then she smiled and said quietly, "I have really good friends. They're everything."

I thought about what it took to be that friend, to support someone whose kid was about to have half of his brain obliterated and I wasn't sure I was up for that task. My own world was heavy enough. But weeks later, after Lydia's son came through the surgery, I listened to her relive the procedure and the brutal days that followed, over lattes and scones. She cried, then I cried, and we eventually ended up laughing and when she was done, she hugged me.

"Thanks. I really needed that."

In the back of my mind, a voice said, "You can be that

friend." I had to admit, I felt privileged listening to her story, one that could have just as easily been my own. I was bearing witness, sharing her fear but, also, her courage.

Right around the same time, Erika's life was spinning into a free fall. She had just brought her third child home from the hospital when her father lost his battle with cancer. I took the two-hour ride to see her, my car packed with her favorite foods, then sat in her driveway, in mute shock. Splintered front steps were held together with a vice-clamp while a screen door dangled by a twisted, rusty wire. Plastic toys dotted the lawn along with gardening tools and shards of clay pots. Inside, kitchen cabinets, like crooked teeth, hung wide open on yellowed walls. Her bathrooms were pockmarked with mold, the bedrooms blanketed in dirty laundry. She was falling apart along with everything else around her.

We sat at her kitchen table and she wept. She was upside down in her mortgage, the bills were piling up, and she missed her Dad. I encouraged her to get out of the house and find a job doing something locally.

"Just get something part-time, something to help stop the bleeding."

"We can't afford the daycare," she sniffed.

"Getting out of the house will do you good. You'll be around people, you'll get on your feet again."

"It's too hard. You don't understand. It's too hard," her sobs ended that conversation and all the conversations we had days, then weeks, later.

She refused therapy and grief counseling. She looked the other way when her kids started showing signs of anxiety. My attempts at helping fell flat. She was looking for validation but I could only offer solutions, action plans, the very things that helped me move through the worst years of my life. I watched as Erika sank further into her depression, unable and unwilling to move from her spot at the table, cigarette in hand, cold coffee in a stained mug. I wasn't sure she would ever recover and then, out of the blue, she invited us for a night out in the city.

"The play is hilarious!" I could sense her smile over the phone. "You'll love it!"

Her husband Mark was a drama teacher and struggling playwright on the side. His play was in previews at a small cabaret and Erika looked gorgeous standing at the front door, flushed with opening night jitters. She hugged me tight, her blond curls circling us like a lace shawl.

"Thank you for coming," she whispered, squeezing my hand. Tears shined in her grey eyes.

"You look amazing," I whispered back, thrilled to see her out and about.

The venue was set up like a dinner theater, cozy and close. We took our seats in the front and then the curtain opened. It was clear from the start that the comedy was not going to be my flavor of funny. The jokes were creaky and dated, more Borsht Belt than 30 Rock. Erika watched for my reaction and I obliged, smiling wildly and laughing at all the right moments.

As if on cue, the waitress appeared with tequila as the humor took a nosedive. "Retard" jokes and riffs about short yellow buses led to the climax, which involved a wheelchair and a punch line about Christopher Reeve. There was more, but I stopped listening as the voices onstage faded into the laughter echoing around me. My ears were finely tuned to the loudest of roars, those coming from Erika and Mark. And in that moment, my heart died just a little bit.

Jay had always taken that short bus to school. And while he could walk without wheelchair assistance, some of his friends could not. There was no amount of tequila that could drown the shame burning up my spine.

As soon as the show ended, my husband and I dashed for the door, yelling hasty goodbyes as we hit the city street.

"Well, now we know." Charlie said quietly, putting the lid on the friendship before I could.

"Yes we do." In fact, I knew so much more than I wanted to. For days after the play, I hit the rewind button, replaying conversations, looking for clues. Erika knew all about my life with Jay, my deep-seated worries and fears, and Mark's play was like a personal nightmare brought to life. Even worse, she invited me to watch and enjoyed every second. I was crushed. And then I was angry.

"So, what did you think of the play?" These were the first words out of her mouth when I answered the phone. I jumped in, head first.

"I'm never going to laugh at a wheelchair joke. Or kids on a short bus."

"It's just Mark's style; obnoxious yes, but just silly fun," she said lightly, as if reviewing the latest Chipmunk movie.

These were Mark's words, his defense, but she was giving them life, standing behind them as if they were her own. Another shock. The aftershock.

"You laughed at someone in a wheelchair! *You* did that!"

"It wasn't personal," she said casually, "Mark certainly didn't mean to offend you. I can't believe you're taking this so seriously."

"I can't believe you're not taking it seriously."

"Jeez, I'm sorry you were hurt by it…" she trailed off.

We spoke a few more times after that, stilted chats made up of polite banter and awkward pauses. I never heard from Mark, someone I had called my friend for more than 10 years, and I never understood Erika's silent defense of his work. I questioned if her free spirit, her "shrug it off" attitude was simply a resistance to stand her ground. Perhaps this was why her life remained in chaos; she refused to make the harder choices, to fight the waves. It was as though I was looking at her for the first time, through a new lens, one without a shared trust or history. And I didn't know what to say to this person, or how to proceed with a friendship that was never really what I thought it was.

So, I avoided her calls, responding with a one or two word text. I resembled every guy I dated in the early '90s—aloof and indifferent. She responded by leaving rambling messages. She had Googled ideas on how to befriend parents of kids with special needs and was ready to start anew. I thought this was funny at first but then my stomach dropped when I realized she actually sought out instruction on how to be my friend.

I flashed back to my chat with Lydia that day in the coffee shop, the tight grip on her napkin while she described her son's recovery. My hand on hers, tears and silent relief. There was no instruction needed.

Then, things went quiet with Erika, both of us retreating to our corners as radio silence replaced our daily chats. I let this happen, knowing we were slipping past the point of no return. I felt paralyzed, unable to let go yet unwilling to hold on. I couldn't just shrug this one off.

Later that month, I spent a weekend with some old friends from high school, girls who can say they knew me when my hair was huge and my jeans were skin-tight and zipped at the ankle. We laughed deep into the night and then started all over the next morning.

It was one of those weekends that flowed easily from start to finish, laughter to tears and back again. Confessionals and declarations, tequila and wine and back again. The simple gesture of a hand over mine, as I talked about Jay's medical struggles, was like salve on a blistered burn. I felt safe in this knowing circle, but most of all, fortified. I saw my reflection in their faces, appreciating the well-earned laugh lines and silvery strands highlighting their temples. In the years since we learned to drive stick shifts together, our shoulders had grown wide and strong. There was great capacity here. There was whispering in the silence, an unspoken mantra of "hell yeah!" when asked to go another round. We were kindred in this way.

On my flight home, I realized that's what was missing with Erika. The way we handled life's biggest challenges, the sleeper waves that hit out of nowhere, had become radically different. She was content to let those waves wash her to shore while I couldn't help but swim against the current. It was suddenly clear to me that our friendship was over, and probably had been for some time.

Yet, I still couldn't think of my younger self without seeing Erika by my side, a touchstone to who I was a million years ago. I loved peeking in that rear view mirror if only to remind myself of how far I'd come. Perhaps that's why I'd tended to our friendship over the years rather than let it go to seed naturally. Ironically enough, that's how it ended anyway.

A few texts here and there, bits of nonsense and gossip, the numbing ointment before the needle. The good news is that I've learned from our breakup. Like all long-term relationships that meet their demise, there is wisdom in the wake.

Now, I'm more careful about who I give my time to. If I'm going to help a friend, she has to be willing to help themselves. To me, the most precious gift of friendship is that support, that hand that reaches out into the darkness. It's like liquid gold poured from one soul to another. Who I share that with reflects who I am, and more importantly, who I hope to become.

These days, when I think of Erika, the memories are sepia-toned and distant. I'll see her smile when a certain Clapton song comes on the radio, reminding me of simpler days. And in those moments I think that maybe I should have told her that our breakup wasn't over a night at the theater, but about who we had grown into and apart from. Maybe I should have called her to the mat, invited her to explain the wheelchair joke to Jay, so she could witness its cruel impact rather than discuss it from atop rhetorical high ground. And maybe, just maybe, she might have experienced that shift from being towed along by the currents to swimming upstream, buoyant and breathless, purposeful and alive, whisper becoming mantra: Hell yeah.

*Alexis is a native New Yorker now living in New Jersey where she works as a Creative Director/Copywriter. In addition to writing ads and web content, she also writes memoir-based essays and is nearly finished with her first book, a YA story about two sisters. Finding the time to write is her biggest challenge so she has reluctantly become a morning person, waking before her two young kids to pound away on her vintage keyboard (it still makes those "clickety" noises) before the light of day. When she's not writing, she can be found running trails with her dog Tilly, hanging out with her husband and kids, and searching for the perfect snack.*

# RECONCILIATIONS

# JESSE LEE

SANDY EBNER

This is how I learned what abuse looks like:

I'm sitting at the bar with Jesse. 19 years old, sipping my Jack and Coke, I think I know everything, so sure I have the world figured out.

"So," I ask her, "why did you and Ronny get a divorce?" Marriage, for me, is a foreign concept, an event likely to occur far into the future, if ever. And so my question to Jesse is asked casually, between drinks, while the band takes a break and we can hear each other talk. Her answer, therefore, comes as a shock.

"He used to beat on me," she says, as calmly as if she's describing a blouse she's planning to buy.

I look at her, unsure how to react. "You mean he beat you, like… he hit you?" She looks back at me, laughing at my naïveté.

"What did you think I meant?" she says, not unkindly.

My friend is beautiful, and men walking by can't help staring. I'm used to this and, for some reason, because it's Jesse I don't care at all. She speaks in a Louisiana dialect that sounds like music. As I sit, trying to think what to say, Jesse tells me her story.

She and Ronny had been married for only a few months when he came home early one morning after spending the night in the bars. This was not, she assures me, an unusual occurrence. I knew that already. It was the 1970s. That's what we all did.

She had waited up for hours before finally going to bed. At dawn he stumbled into their bedroom and shook her awake, demanding that she make him breakfast. He smelled like perfume. Instead of confronting him—like I would, I think—she got out of bed and made him a plate of eggs. This surprises me. After growing up in Northern California, where women's rights were debated constantly, I think about what I would say. *Make your own breakfast, asshole.*

Ronny sat at their kitchen table, took two bites and said, "This is shit."

Jesse got mad, naturally, complaining that not only had she just cooked him breakfast but that he'd been out all night without so much as a phone call and, apparently, from the smell of him, with another woman. Ronny stood up and threw the plate of food in her face. And then he punched her.

"This happened all the time," she says. "Eventually he just left me." I couldn't believe what I was hearing. *He* left?

Being young and single, my ideas about marriage are as remote from reality as they can possibly be. But, I think, at least I know what marriage will *not* look like. I won't be serving breakfast on demand to anybody, much less a man who has just spent the night with someone other than me.

All I manage in response is a pitifully inadequate, "Oh

God, Jesse. That sucks." (Or words to that effect.) Such is life when you are young and stupid.

At this point in my life, I have never met anyone who'd experienced anything like what she was describing. (Later, of course, I would learn that I had, they just never talked about it.) My parents never fought in front of my sisters and me. None of the men I dated—or slept with—ever raised their voices to me, much less hit me. Sadly, this would change, and eventually I would come to understand Jesse in a much clearer way. But as she told me her story it was as if she were speaking a different language. I was shocked, not just because this seemed to be a normal experience for her, but mostly because I couldn't understand why she would allow herself to be abused.

I first met Jesse in the summer of 1976. I don't remember how, probably in a bar, but we soon became inseparable. We worked at different clubs, but we saw each other as often as we could, after our respective shifts, or on our nights off.

The differences between us didn't seem like much, but she was a local, raised in the rural south, and I wasn't. Sadly, this meant that our lives would take very separate paths.

When I moved back to California, not long after Jesse told me her story, we assumed we'd see each other again soon. The morning I left we stood on her front lawn taking snapshots until it was time for me to go, Jesse with her boyfriend Dan, who would become her second husband, and Trina, her daughter from her marriage with Ronny.

She was living in what would turn out to be one in a

long line of rundown houses she would live in over the course of her life: an old shotgun house with holes in the floor, a leaky roof, and appliances that only occasionally worked. Filled with mismatched furniture and a single mattress on the living room floor, it was not the kind of house I ever planned on living in, but then neither had she.

I wouldn't see Jesse again for eight years. But during that time I heard from her often.

The first time she calls it is long past midnight. I answer the phone and hear someone crying. Disoriented, I try to think who might be calling at this hour.

"Who is this?" I begin to panic, thinking it might be one of my sisters, that something has happened to one of our parents.

Jesse mumbles something then, between sobs, and I finally recognize her voice.

"Jesse?" I say. "What's wrong?" She doesn't answer, just continues to cry.

"Jesse. What happened?"

"He beat me again," she says.

"Who? *Dan?*" I'm stunned. I introduced Dan to Jesse, thinking they might be suited to one another.

"Where is he?" I finally ask.

"Gone. Probably to New Orleans." Of course he is, I think. The bars in New Orleans stay open all night.

"Jesse," I say. "I'm so sorry." Meaningless words that won't do a thing to help her, but they are the best I can do from 2,000 miles away. And so I lie there, half asleep, and listen to her cry.

After that, the calls come regularly, every few months, and our relationship begins to develop a disturbing pattern. I answer the phone and hear her cries.

"He hit me," she says, and again I listen to her sobs, again not knowing what to say. I am horrified that my friend is in pain, but after the first few calls my responses become rote, as if I am following a script: "Where is he now?" I say. "Is Trina okay?"

She and Dan have two daughters together, but eventually they divorce. And yet the calls keep coming. Each time, we have the same conversation but one involving an entirely different person. Dan. Jimmy. Charlie. They beat her, she says, or punched her, or kicked her, or threw her against a wall. *Who would do these things?* I think. A lot of people apparently, judging from Jesse's calls. I begin to wonder if this might be a cultural thing.

These phone calls, for a time, become the basis of our friendship. Someone will beat her, and she will call me; someone else will beat her, and she will call me again; on and on, year after year. Each time we talk I feel utterly helpless. There is nothing I can do but listen, let her cry, tell her that I love her, until she is too tired to stay on the phone any longer. *Why don't you just leave?* I say. I beg her to take the children and go to her mother's house, or anywhere that she will be safe. Sometimes she would. But she always went back.

*** 

Several years later, no longer as naïve as I once was, I realized there were likely to be more complicated reasons why Jesse stayed in abusive relationships beyond the fact that she had three children to care for. But by then I was beginning to get angry. I had gone through some difficult years myself, and was tired of always being there for her. When had she been there for me when I needed someone?

What could I do for her if she wasn't willing to help herself? This was how my mind worked back then.

Over time she seemed to accept this life as her due. Often I heard her say, "Well, at least he's not hitting me right now," when she talked about her boyfriend, or husband, as if that alone made him a good person. I'd heard other southern women say the same thing, as if this were normal behavior, something you put up with in order to have a man in your life. I was disgusted by this, not understanding it at all. I couldn't conceive of being in that situation even once, much less multiple times.

As Jesse got older her relationships, thankfully, became less volatile. The late night calls lessened, then finally stopped. For the next few years we talked at Christmas or on birthdays. We wrote each other often, signing our letters with an acronym: YBFITWEW, *Your Best Friend in the Whole Entire World.* Corny, maybe, but it was a habit we'd started when we were young. (Thirty years later, we still sign our letters that way.) Eventually, though, we had such different lives, and were separated by so many miles, that our letters became scarce.

Over the years I visited Louisiana now and then, and when I did we would see each other in the French Quarter, or in the town where we'd first met. But by now my view of our relationship had changed. I had come to see it as selfish, one-sided. Why was it always up to me to take the initiative? I always went to her. I always paid for dinner. I always took her to New Orleans. *I, I, I.* It's painful to look back now and realize that I was the selfish one.

Jesse's girls grew up and started families of their own. I married and settled into a stable, happy life. I thought of her often, but never made much effort to maintain the friendship. But, I reasoned, neither did she.

***

My circumstances changed when my mother moved to the Gulf Coast, which meant that when I visited her I was only a short drive away from Jesse. But, as it turns out, I rarely took the time to make the drive. Her life always seemed to be in a perpetual state of crisis. Her phone was cut off regularly, which left her impossible to reach. I had a hard time summoning up the energy required to find her, and felt a twinge of guilt each time I got on the plane to fly home, vowing that I would see her next time. But as each trip came and went I always found another excuse not to seek out my old friend, until last year when I flew down to visit my mother for Christmas.

It is after the holiday, and I have several days before returning home. One morning I grow restless, and I tell my mother I'm going out to look up some old friends. Perhaps I'll try to see Jesse but I'm not sure I'll be able to find her or if I even want to. As usual, I have no phone number for her, no way to know where she is living.

When I get to the small town where I hope she still lives, I drive to the last address I have for her. An old duplex with peeling paint and barred windows, the place looks the same as every other house she'd lived in, which is to say deeply depressing. A chain-link fence separates the house from the one next door, and two plastic chairs sit next to the porch steps, an ashtray on the ground between them. Despite the knot in my stomach I get out of the car and walk to the front door, half hoping no one is home. I knock, and after a moment an older man opens the door. He looks wary, clearly assuming I'm there trying to sell something.

"I'm looking for Jesse," I say.

He hesitates, but opens the door a bit wider. Finally he says, "Yeah. Come on in." I follow him into a house filled, literally, with junk. A mattress is upended against one wall, and boxes are haphazardly stacked everywhere. A filthy overstuffed chair, presumably vacated by the same man who had answered the door, sits across from a small TV, the volume turned low.

He motions for me to follow, and leads me to a closed door at the back of the house. He knocks and says, "Hey Jesse. You've got a visitor."

It's almost noon and she's still sleeping? Either she worked late the night before, or she's still involved with a lifestyle I had long ago given up.

"Jesse!" He knocks again. "Someone's here to see you." Then the door opens, and there she is. Groggy from sleep, it takes her a moment to recognize me. When she does, she starts to cry. We hug each other for a long time, both of us crying now.

"What are you doing here?" she asks.

"I drove over from Waveland," I say. "I had no way to reach you." I hug her again, surprised to realize how much I've missed her. A man standing behind her looks at me as if he knows who I am. "You must be Sandy," he says.

Jesse turns towards him and smiles. "This is my husband, Tom," she says. Husband? This man looks young enough to be her son. *Nothing ever changes,* I think.

We make small talk for a while, but finally I ask if she might like to get some lunch. The house is making me claustrophobic and I'm beginning to feel anxious. I don't know Tom, or the man who answered the door, but I know one of them is selling drugs. Several men have come and gone already in the short time I've been here, each of them taking a turn in the bathroom. I know what a drug house looks like. I can only assume Jesse is also using.

She gets dressed and we walk downtown to find a place to eat. We sit at the bar and talk, laughing about things we'd done together, our times behind the bar, the friends and customers we'd known.

"They used to call me 'Swamp,' remember?" Jesse says.

"Who did?" I say, confused.

"Oh, my regulars, because of where I was born. They never meant anything by it."

"But why?" I ask. "Ponchatoula's not the swamp."

"I was born in Manchac," she says. "I didn't move to Ponchatoula until later."

"I never knew that."

Manchac was out in the bayous between New Orleans and Baton Rouge, a place you passed on the way to somewhere else. There was a famous seafood restaurant there, at least famous in south Louisiana.

The gap in meaning between 'bayou' and 'swamp' couldn't possibly be wider, and it has nothing at all to do with their geographical differences. One is romantic and mysterious, while the other conjures up images of poor white trash, which to some people is just about the worst thing you can be.

She hadn't been trying to hide this. She must have known I wouldn't care one way or the other. It had just, surprisingly, never come up.

"My father threw my mother out of the house when I was five," she says.

"Your mother in Ponchatoula?"

"That's my stepmother. She's the one who raised me. My real mother lives in Amite. I've only met her a couple times." Amite is a small town less than twenty miles from where we were sitting.

She tells me her father beat her mother for years, eventually throwing her out of her own house, taking their young daughter for himself. As she says this, I think about all the late night phone calls. My burger sits untouched in front of me as she describes her hellish childhood, one that I now knew had become a template for her entire life.

Now, many years later, she has no money and no medical insurance. She is no longer able to work. Several years before, she had been diagnosed with Hepatitis C, and suffered from debilitating bouts with fibromyalgia. She has no car, and is dependent on anybody who can take her where she needs to go that is farther than walking distance from the house. Her daughters live nearby but refuse to see her. I ask why, and she says it's because they dislike Tom. I suspect it has more to do with her drug use, but I say nothing.

She lived under appalling conditions, which I'd seen just a glimpse of. She and Tom rarely had enough to eat. They shared the house with his father, who Tom had only met recently. This was, apparently, the man who had answered the door. He spent all day, Jesse said, in front of the TV. He paid half the rent, but also stole their food, and anything else they left lying around. They had no privacy, padlocking the door to their bedroom when they left the house to protect the few possessions they had. They were virtual prisoners in a house most people wouldn't want to step foot in, much less live .

That night, I took her to New Orleans, because it was the only thing I could think of to do for her. We walked the streets of the Quarter, eating beignets and buying silly trinkets, things that tourists do. I took her to dinner at a restaurant that, in hindsight, must have made her uncomfortable. She looked at the menu and I saw that she was afraid to make a choice, faced with entrees that cost more money than she could ever spend on one meal. But I also saw that she was struggling to have fun, something she hadn't done in a very long time. She tasted goat cheese for the first time, and drank two glasses of expensive Chardonnay. We laughed and laughed, as the friend I had loved for so long let go of her pain, if only for a few hours.

The next day, instead of goat cheese and risotto, we drank sweet tea and ate oyster Po-boys. That night, we stood on the hotel balcony in the cold, watching the tourists laughing below.

"You know what I want?" she said, as she lit a cigarette and watched the lights of the city. "All I want is a trailer of my own, and enough room for a garden."

My old prejudices bubbled up again. You want to live in a *trailer?* Why not dream for a house, I wondered, or at least a house with a shower that worked or a front door that locked?

Later, as I listened to her softly snoring in the bed next to mine, I thought, how did I escape this? A life where the most you can hope for is a trailer on the side of a two-lane highway? Even with all the problems I'd had in my own life, it had been a winning lottery ticket compared to what my friend had lived with.

I felt my resentment towards her begin to disappear, my anger at her for not being there when I needed her, for continuing to let men abuse her. My ignorance had colored my view of our relationship for so long that I had been unable to see the truth. There were many times I had not been Jesse's friend, and she hadn't been mine.

The difference is that I felt as if, somehow, I should have known better. Because of the advantages I'd had, perhaps, because I'd had an easier life, because I was the lucky one.

I watched her as she slept and suddenly, at the oddest of times, I realized that what Jesse had given me over the years was something for which I would never be able to adequately thank her: friendship and unconditional love. Why had it taken me so long to recognize such a simple thing?

*** 

Six months later, she calls me again. She's going into rehab. Her daughters are insisting, saying it is the only way she'll ever see her grandchildren. She and Tom have separated because he is unwilling to give up the drugs, and that night I think, not for the first time, *how much can one person endure?*

As I hang up the phone, I think about how lucky I am to have had her as my friend, and how if I could do only one thing for her, besides love her, I would buy her the one small thing she wants out of life: a trailer, with a garden. A place of her own that no one can take from her, a place where I will always be able to find her.

*Author's Note: Not long after this piece was accepted for publication in* My Other Ex, *Jesse died unexpectedly. I am profoundly grateful that I reconnected with her before her death. While I am saddened by her loss, I look back on our friendship not with regret but with a sense of peace. Due to the subject matter, all names in this essay have been changed, except for my own.*

*"Jesse Lee" was previously published in* The Dead Mule

School of Southern Literature *and* The Dr. T.J. Eckleburg Review.

*Sandy Ebner lives and writes in Northern California. Her essays have been published or are forthcoming in the* San Francisco Chronicle, Connotation Press: An Online Artifact, Dead Mule School of Southern Literature, The Doctor T.J. Eckleburg Review, *and other publications. She writes about a variety of topics, but is most interested in social and cultural differences and how they influence our lives. Her essay, 'The Clothes I Was Wearing' was named a finalist in both the 2012 Press 53 Open Awards and the 2012 Glass Woman Prize, in addition to being nominated by Connotation Press for a Pushcart Prize. She holds a Bachelor's Degree in Journalism from Cal State University, and is an alumna of the Community of Writers at Squaw Valley. She currently serves as Creative Nonfiction Editor at MadHat Lit and MadHat Annual (Mad Hatter's Review) and is working on her first novel.*

# ERASED

---

ANDREA NEUSNER

We are winding our way through the dusty roads of Jerusalem in her tiny car. She's picked me up from my spare rental apartment and we're speeding through the maze of streets in this, her adopted city.

It isn't supposed to happen this way. Not on her turf. Not in her car. She's even chosen the restaurant; it's her country. The words are right behind my eyes, because I've practiced them for years. In my imagination, I've spit them out in a vacuum, without a setting. But here we are, in Jerusalem of all places, and the sun is setting, the buildings awash in its golden glow.

It is my first trip to Israel since a semester here in college, 20 years ago, right around the time that we last spoke.

At first, I announce my month long trip on Facebook, willing her to take the bait. She does.

*When?*

*Are you really coming?*

*Can I see you?*

I send her a message back.

*Yes.*

Her next message has her email, street address, home number and cell, with instructions to call her when I get to Israel.

I don't call when I arrive. I'm not ready to hear her voice. I email instead. We arrange to have dinner the following week, and, finally, the day before our dinner, I call her home number. We make a plan, though I don't recognize the voice on the other end.

But when that face shows up at my door, there is no mistaking her. She is simultaneously familiar and foreign, the physical embodiment of déjà vu.

She parks the car a few blocks away and as we walk towards the restaurant, we cut through swarms of children playing in a park, and our conversation becomes fast and easy. We are filling in the lost years—jobs, marriages, and children.

In front of the restaurant there's an outdoor grill sizzling with meat. The aromas are intoxicating.

The call to prayer momentarily interrupts our conversation. Its mournfulness reminds me of the reason I agreed to this dinner—to finally confront her about our lost friendship. At that moment I wish to be Muslim so I could pause for a few moments of reflection.

Facing each other in the restaurant, I can't stop staring at her face. Twenty years. She has wrinkles now. And spots of sun damage are sprinkled across her face from the harsh Israeli sun.

We went through Jewish Day School and then Hebrew high school together. "We grew apart," I told our high school crowd, who couldn't believe that once inseparable best friends no longer spoke. But it was true. While she grew serious, religious, and dreamed of moving to Israel, I pledged a sorority. She spent Friday nights observing the Sabbath. My Friday night ritual was dancing in some dive bar. I was having fun. I knew that I was being judged by her. And I didn't care. By the end of college she stopped returning my phone calls.

I wish there had been a blowout. I think that might have been easier than just being erased. Everyone understands what an argument is. Instead, I was slowly wounded. When we were both home for visits, she didn't make time for me.

On one of these visits, after phoning her several times to get together, there was this response:

"Well, I'm busy right now, but I've got to go to CVS. I guess you could come for that."

CVS? I could accompany her to CVS? This was someone I spent every Saturday night with for years. We had a language all our own. We'd sometimes write out lists of our inside jokes, and would marvel at how nearly everything triggered some private memory we shared. We had what I'd later learn spouses have, where we could read each other's minds with a look or glance.

Saturday nights had had their own rhythm. Dinner, bake brownies, then "Love Boat" and "Fantasy Island." Bed. When the lights went out we told each other everything, her whispering from her bed, and me from the cot that her dad rolled in for me each week.

I don't remember anything more about the CVS conversation, only that it was my official dismissal from her life.

I wish I had taken the hint. I tried a few more times in vain to make plans, and it took people who loved me—newer friends who didn't know our history—to tell me I was being kind of pathetic, chasing this woman from my girlhood past. I could not let go. Letting go would feel like erasing my childhood and teenage years. She was the witness to my life. If my witness was gone, did the past exist? Did I?

Then I was invited to her wedding, but I didn't go. On the RSVP card I made a litany of paltry excuses. At least, I thought, the cord would be cut. When I next visited home and ran into her parents, they treated me as though I were invisible.

Now the grown woman in her forties in front of me has crow's feet and a deep tan. She's a teacher, in a special school for Arab and Jewish children, where they learn side by side in both Hebrew and Arabic.

I'm enjoying her company. She is warm and funny, interesting and off beat—all the things I once loved about her.

I am searching for my prepared script, but I am at a loss. There are no calculated words, just tears lying in wait. If she brings it up I will crumple.

She orders us salads and grilled fish in perfect Hebrew. As I hand over my menu, her tanned face smiles at me, and this time I see years well lived. I surprise myself by being happy for her accomplishments—a beautiful family, a job she loves, and the successful move to Israel, where life is not always easy.

As we eat, I describe the details of my current life, and she shares her stories with me.

The bill comes, and dinner is nearly over. It is clear she will not bring up the past. She will not apologize. If I have something to say, I'm running out of time. My need to confront her has vanished and it dawns on me that no matter what has happened I will not hurt her. Instead what I am thinking about is the Shehechiyanu blessing.

"Blessed are You Lord our God, Ruler of the Universe who has given us life, sustained us, and allowed us to reach this day."

I am simply pleased to be sharing a meal with my old friend, in this beautiful city, where battles have raged for centuries. The one gift I can give the both of us, right here, right now, is peace.

*Andrea Neusner lives in Washington DC with her husband and three daughters. Her work has been published in* Seltzer *and* The Huffington Post. *She is a regular contributor to* Delight Gluten-Free Magazine.

# A FRIENDSHIP IN TIME

ESTELLE ERASMUS

*After breaking up*—the *distance between me and Laura, and the passing of the years*—*only made our bond of friendship deeper once we reunited.*

I met Laura at the office where we both worked for a women's magazine: my job was in editorial, hers in advertising sales. For both of us it was "like" at first sight, though we were very different in appearance, attitude, and personal situation.

I was brunette, curvy, Jewish, and book smart; not sure of my own value; practically engaged to a man I thought I loved, but didn't like that much, with whom I stayed out of a sense of misguided loyalty and not a little fear.

Laura was a few years older than me, blonde, slim-hipped, a non-practicing Catholic divorcee; single, wild and free; dating a separated, married man, who spent money on her lavishly.

My job as a Senior Editor was low-paying, but I loved working in the publishing industry, going to press events, traveling around the country to review hotels and spas, writing columns, interviewing celebrities and finding books to excerpt in the publication. I joked with my friends and family that I was perk rich but cash poor.

Not so my boyfriend. He came from a well-to-do family rife with dysfunction—and relatives constantly jockeying for position—a situation that had a horrifying resemblance to a Tennessee Williams novel. In between his mood swings he was charming and doting, telling me how much he loved me, but verbally attacking me when we would fight—mostly about his family and how they controlled him.

Though we were practically engaged (I know he had bought a ring), I tried to ignore the anxiety I felt at the thought of marriage, which had me waking, gasping for breath, from nightmares of being smothered.

Laura enthralled me. She was a gourmet-dining, fine-wine drinking, wisecracking woman with the ability to finesse any situation and transfix any man with her green eyes and come-hither stare. She was also surprisingly spiritual, saying you attract what you put out, and she regularly tithed a percentage of her paycheck to charity. She had a worldly mien, particularly about men, that I sorely lacked.

She reminded me of my "aunt" Clara from childhood—my great-uncle Kalman's girlfriend—who was blonde, free-spirited, with a lush mouth unfailingly decorated with hot pink lipstick and a ready, boisterous laugh. They would take me to Coney Island, where we'd ride the rollercoaster and eat ice cream cones, watching our careless dribbles evaporate as they hit the hot pavement.

I wasn't consciously aware of it, but I craved someone to take me away from the safe, somewhat limited world I inhabited, where everyone behaved properly, and waited for men to make the first move. Laura created her own rules and lived within them brilliantly: a siren's lure to someone like me.

I tried to please other people and felt I was always furiously (exhaustingly) pedaling below the surface to give myself the appearance of a swan, but inside I felt more like a clumsy, awkward duck. My inner peace was missing, and sometimes I felt so bound up in ambition that it tangled me inside, because wasn't it wrong to be ambitious? Wasn't it bad to exploit my looks to get what I needed? Laura didn't think so.

Like a Zen master, with me as her pupil, she taught me the ways of men, money, and self-worth.

"You must be so excited that you're getting married soon," Laura told me not too soon after we first met.

"I guess. I'm not sure," I ventured.

"Do you love him?" she asked me.

"I don't know. I don't think so," I offered sadly.

"Well, if you don't love him why are you still with him?" she asked indignantly.

That night I thought long and hard about my life. Why indeed was I with someone whom I didn't quite respect, or really love? Was I just going through the motions? Laura made me question my choices. Within a week of this reckoning, I broke up with the man. I have never regretted that decision.

One day, she gave me tips on making the most of my looks. "You have great boobs. You need to work it," she said while we were out shopping. I was accustomed to finding my tasteful, fitted dresses downtown at vintage clothing stores, like the Antique Boutique, but under Laura's tutelage, I let the sex bomb in me flow, and joined her in wearing mini skirts with wide belts to accentuate my slim waist, hot red lipstick, and knee-high black boots along with tight-fitting V-neck tops that showed just a hint of cleavage. Laura and I enjoyed the spoils of her generous client account as we dined and drank and flirted with single (and possibly married) men at fine restaurants all over the city. I perfected the art of flirting, getting male attention as she did by using a subtle smile and nod of the head (I was still too shy to use the direct stare that was Laura's Scorpio trademark).

I grew accustomed to the stares and wolf whistles Laura and I would attract when we'd walk down the street and enjoyed our daily ritual of taking the elevator down to the first floor café, where we'd get our customary free chocolate chip muffin tops from the admiring, male wait staff.

I was there for her when she broke up with the separated, married man she was dating, and commiserated as she put on Gloria Gaynor's "I Will Survive," and we danced and drank and cried and laughed, the laugh of survivors in love till the early hours of the night.

Later, when I was considering working for another publisher, they asked me to do some work on spec. When I told Laura, she said, "Estelle, they need to pay you. You should never work for free." Bolstered by her support, I asked for and received a generous fee for my work.

She was my mentor, my friend, my drinking (okay, I was a lightweight) and partying buddy, but because I was unsure of my own worth, I never thought I was her equal.

I tried to repay her generosity and friendship in kind. I took her to movie screenings and gave her beauty products and other swag that I received. But after a few years, the climate changed at the magazine and I started to look for another job.

Around the same time, Laura found her soul mate: A Midwest-transplant who was a physician. They married; I found a new job. All of a sudden, the pursuits we used to share had no appeal to Laura. She was madly in love and settling into married life. She didn't drive so she couldn't come see me in New Jersey, and I wasn't comfortable hanging out with her and her husband in Queens.

We were at an impasse, and as friends on different paths often do, we lost touch. It was gradual, but slowly the woman who had been so important to me slid out of my life like the sands in an hourglass.

And time marched on. I learned how to value myself more and more with each failed relationship; figured out how to stand up for myself; increased my income exponentially; found the courage to bravely take on a job that entailed driving 80 miles a day; changed careers and then changed back again; wrote a best-selling book that is still in print; contributed to several anthologies; traveled the world; conquered most of my insecurities from childhood; lost my naiveté; gained worldliness; and finally in midlife met the man I loved, lived with and then married (and never once had a dream that I was suffocating).

Flash-forward 14 years from the time we last saw each other—I am pregnant, in my third trimester. I call Laura, because I've been reaching out to people in my past and sharing my joy. And, mostly I call her because I've been thinking of her and how she has been such a strong influence in my life.

She picks up on the second ring. "How are you, Estelle

Sobel?" she said. "I saw your name on the phone and I couldn't believe it."

"I'm great, Laura. I'm actually Estelle Sobel Erasmus now. I'm married...and pregnant."

"Do you know what you are having?"

"Yes, we're having a girl."

"That is fantastic!" she yelled into the phone. "I'm so happy for you. I was hoping you had gotten married. But you are also going to have a baby. This is so great."

"I want to see you," she said. "What are you doing next week?"

We get together the following week, and the minute I see her, I instantly feel our old connection. We talk all through our lunch, and though I am cautiously optimistic, she is all in, which feels wonderful to pregnant, hormonal me.

And this time around we are both settled in our lives. And most importantly, in my mind, we are on equal footing because I finally know my own worth.

Today, almost five years later, Laura is my closest friend.

We are both happily married, and we both are stay at home wives (she doesn't work, and I work from home as a freelance writer, editor, and blogger able to make my own schedule). The days when we would go out on the town, flirting and drinking and dancing are long behind us. We are glad we had those days, but we are happy that they are over now.

Since the birth of my daughter, Laura (who by choice has remained childless) has driven to New Jersey to see us every week, without fail, no matter what the weather. Yes, in the years between us, Laura has learned how to drive.

Of all my friends, my daughter knows Laura the best

because Laura has seen her on a weekly basis since she was born. Laura, in turn, is my daughter's biggest fan. She even learned how to diaper and bottle-feed my daughter to give me a break and would help me lug my daughter's heavy stroller wherever we needed to go. In those early days of motherhood, seeing Laura in the middle of every week was a treat for me, and I looked forward to it like the earth craves rain in the midst of a draught. Laura was dealing with the difficulty of caretaking for her mom, and she, too, looked forward to taking a vacation from the worry.

The fabric of our friendship has grown more textured: where once we man-shopped, now we food shop (and share tips on the best smoked salmon). Where we used to look for the sexiest clothing, now we scan the aisles for high quality, classic-looking sweaters, shoes, and accessories. Where we used to commiserate over men, we now connect over the challenges of raising a girl in a male-dominated world.

When I couldn't shake my Red Bull addiction shortly after giving birth, Laura was the one who pointed out its chemicals and high sugar content. When Laura shows me a dress that she wants to buy that is more like something a teenage girl would wear, I gently (*okay, not so gently*), steer her towards a more age-appropriate item. She returns the favor by guiding me away from the sequin sweaters I crave.

During our friendship break, we both moved away from a self-centered world-view, and now discuss politics with the passion that we used to feel gossiping about the ex-girlfriends of the men we were dating. I watched Laura become a dedicated caretaker to her mother, during the last years of her mom's life, and sat by her side at her mother's wake. She, in turn, came with me to visit my dad when he was in the hospital after breaking his hip. And it's Laura with whom I share my not-so-proud mom moments and it's she who reassures me that I'm doing a great job and that I am raising my daughter the right way. And Laura relies on me as her emotional anchor, in a way that she has been unable to do with her closest living relatives.

Admittedly, it is an intense friendship (we *both* have strong personalities this time around), but I now know how important I am to Laura, and how essential we are to each other. We had a major fight a few years ago, and Laura, who came from an unstable family, thought our friendship was over, because that was her experience growing up. But our friendship was too important to me to lose, and I let her know that, while also standing my ground. In the process, I taught her that we are never going to break up again. As a result, she trusts me more than she has ever trusted anyone in her life, with the exception of her husband. I honor that trust and return it.

I couldn't imagine my life without Laura; I couldn't imagine taking another break from our friendship, and thankfully neither can she. I'm grateful for the years we had between us, where we focused on developing ourselves and building stable lives, and I firmly believe, as does Laura, that our relationship is richer for the break we took from each other.

*Estelle Erasmus is a journalist, author and former magazine editor who has contributed to several anthologies, including The ASJA Guide to Freelance Writing (St. Martin's Press) and What Do Mothers Need? Motherhood Activists and Scholars Speak Out on Maternal Empowerment for the 21st Century (Demeter*

*Press). Estelle writes about her transformative journey through midlife motherhood with a young daughter on her blog Musings On Motherhood & Midlife (http://musingsonmotherhoodmidlife.com) and at the* Huffington Post. *Her essays have been published on* Marie Claire, Working Mother, The New York Daily News, Project Eve, Kveller, Erma Bombeck Writers' Workshop, *and syndicated on* BlogHer. *She is a 2014 and 2012 BlogHer Voice of the Year, and a member of the inaugural New York City 2012 production of* Listen to Your Mother.

# THE INTERNET BREAKUP

ALISON LEE

"Have a good life."

That sentence ended the last email I wrote to my former best online friend. It spoke volumes of my anger and pain.

Mandy and I clicked immediately. I had only been blogging for a few months when we met, and for two years, our friendship grew from strength to strength. We were as far apart geographically as one can imagine (nearly 10,000 miles), her morning was my night, my morning, her night. We were of different faiths and backgrounds. We couldn't have been more different. And yet we couldn't have been more similar. We had the same sense of humor, similar life values, and the same brutal honesty. I could talk to her about everything. She was my safe landing place.

Online relationships are written about often in blog posts and articles. We talk about how they are as real as the relationships we build in our off-line lives. We write about how we invest our emotions and time in people we only know through their words, and avatars. We watch those people grow as writers, mothers, daughters, wives, sisters. We watch their children grow up, and we share in their milestones.

We celebrate their joys—marriages, pregnancies, births, successful adoptions, job promotions, book launches, new businesses. We hold their virtual hands, and offer virtual shoulders when they suffer losses, divorce, breakups, failures. We pray and cheer for each other. We cry and laugh together. We introduce each other to mutual friends. We start businesses and write books together. We form private Facebook groups, sharing our inner-most thoughts and opinions. We form Google Plus Communities together, to bring other like-minded folk into the circle.

We become Facebook friends. We exchange phone numbers. We Skype. We chat on Google Hangout. We call and text each other on the telephone. Some of us even meet these online friends, crossing the line into real-life friends. And if we're so lucky, we start hanging out with them, and their families. We meet each other's spouses and partners. We meet their children. We take photos together and share them on Instagram. We go out for dinner together and arrange playdates for our kids (and ourselves). We give each other gifts on birthdays and Christmas.

We are fully invested in these friendships. They are real. They are in our circle of trust, the circle of "I want to tell you this before anyone else," the circle of "I know only you will understand this."

Mandy and I were in each other's circles. Other than my husband, she was the first person I told about my much-awaited second pregnancy. She excitedly shared her own pregnancy news with me six weeks later. She was the one I confided in during the difficult first six months of mothering two children, and she turned to me when things became chaotic in her household of six. We supported each other when we both started our own businesses. We were thick as thieves.

But sadly, just as in real life, sometimes the friendship wavers, and something happens (a misunderstanding, a miscommunication, *something*), when words are exchanged heatedly, and you cross another line, one that you never imagined you'd come to. You **break up**.

Our "something" came in the form of the different blogging and social media paths that we had begun to take, away from each other. She wanted to slow down, focus on other things. I was keen to explore new writing opportunities outside of my blog, and grow my social media consulting business. She felt neglected (she probably was), and I felt unsupported. The tiny cracks in our friendship became a huge rift. We said awful things to each other. Accusations were thrown around.

And then came that final email to Mandy, "Have a good life." We broke up.

It felt as real as a real-life friendship breakup. You would think that since you only really know each other online (especially if you live oceans apart, and have never met), it would be easier. You don't have to worry about bumping into her at the grocery store, or avoiding eye contact at school pickup. You don't have to worry about sitting at the same table at a mutual friend's wedding, or rearranging carpooling duties so you don't have to pick each other's kids up for team sports.

No. It is not easy. It is not easy even if you decide to stop following her on Twitter and Instagram, and "unfriend" her on Facebook. Inevitably, you will see her on someone's blog, having left the comment before yours. You will see her on Twitter because someone retweeted her funny update. You will see her liking someone's photo on Instagram. You will see her guest posting on a blog you both read.

You admit that yes, occasionally, you go to her blog to lurk, just to see how she is, and what she's been up to. You click on her Twitter feed to do the same. You try to ask a mutual friend, casually, whether they've heard from her, and if she's asked about you. You wonder if she's doing the same—lurking on *your* blog, checking on *your* Twitter feed. You wonder if she misses you as much as you miss her. You wonder if just like you, she realizes with a pang that she no longer has you to ping when she has something she wants to tell someone. You wonder if she's hurting as much as you are. You wonder if she wishes that maybe someday, you can be friends again.

So yes, online breakups are real. Just as online friendships are.

For nine long months, I missed Mandy. From talking daily to not talking at all, it was as if a hole had opened up in my heart. The gaping void did not diminish with time. I rehashed our conversations and email exchanges, wondering if I had made a mistake in severing our friendship.

Many good things happened to me in 2013. But the breakup weighed heavily on me, and cast a shadow over all the good. I missed my friend, and I felt guilty for my part in what happened. I did not want the year to end on that note.

I reached out in a tentative email, apologizing for all

that transpired, and offered an olive branch. I asked for forgiveness and a second chance.

She replied. Our year ended as the year began—as friends. Our initial correspondence was timid. We asked each other casual questions, how are you, how are the children. We started chatting again on Twitter. Our friendship was back on track within weeks.

As much as I wish we didn't have to break up, I know that this hurdle in our friendship has strengthened us in many ways. We know what cannot break us, and we now realize the depth of our love and respect for each other.

*Mandy is not her real name.

*Alison Lee is a former PR and marketing professional turned work-at-home mother. After a 10-year career in various PR agencies, and of the world's biggest sports brands, Alison traded in launch parties, product launches, international press junkets and world travel, for sippy cups and diapers, breastfeeding and potty training. Alison has been actively over-sharing stories of motherhood on her blog, Writing, Wishing since 2011. Her writing has also been featured on* The Huffington Post, Mamalode, Queen Latifah, *and* Scary Mommy. *She is a weekly blogger at* Everyday Family *and founder of social media consulting business,* Little Love Media, *specializing in working with bloggers, self-published authors, and small businesses. Alison lives in Kuala Lumpur, Malaysia with her husband, two boys and is expecting boy/ girl twins in October 2014.*

# LUCK AND FORGIVENESS

HALLIE SAWYER

I've never been very good at friendships. If anything, I feel as if the most important relationships in my life were based on luck. When I was nine, I landed in the same class as my future best friend. When we were paired together for a class project, all the other girls in my grade seemed to fade away, as if they were out of focus. We clung to each other as we navigated our way away from the cracks of our dysfunctional upbringing.

Later in college, luck was there for me again when I joined a sorority, which gave me over a hundred friends before classes even started. I met Jennifer during the first week of sorority rush as we both pledged the same house. When she told me she had a younger sister named Hallie, I took it as a sign. As friends during that freshman year, we didn't have to initiate plans, activities were planned for us. When we moved into the sorority house, we didn't really have to work at our friendship. Proximity did the work for us and, most of the time, all we had to do was show up.

During those years, we celebrated birthdays, wept over boyfriends, crammed for exams, and killed a few brain cells together. I even traveled home with Jennifer once or twice to spend the weekend with her family. I considered her one of my best friends, which was a pretty small crowd.

After graduation, we both got jobs in Omaha; Jennifer as a junior high art teacher and I ended up as a recruiter with a technical staffing firm. It was a no-brainer to move in together, but little did I know that this was the beginning of a year-long breakup.

Late in my college career, I had met my future husband. It wasn't until the last semester of college that we became serious. When I moved to Omaha for my job, he was still finishing up his senior year. I was immersed in my new job, Jennifer in hers, and all was well. Or so I thought.

When I wasn't busy in my new corporate life, I was off frolicking in love. This first crack in our friendship was caused by the proximity of my boyfriend and the vast distance of hers. Mine was located only 45 minutes away, while hers was two states away in Texas. I left most weekends to go see my boyfriend. She did not. Occasionally she would fly down or he would fly home, but it was nowhere near the same. As my relationship intensified—I got engaged that Christmas and, of course, asked Jennifer to be a bridesmaid—hers struggled to stay afloat.

As I spun between my busy work week and my boyfriend weekends, I didn't realize I was slowly shutting her out. It wasn't very surprising since every aspect of our lives seemed to be in conflict. Along with the boyfriend disparity, our daily lives were drastically different. She was home by four o'clock every day, while I was taking a coffee break at about that time before I put in another three hours of phone calls and interviews. I was either hanging out with co-workers after work, having drinks like it was College 2.0, or cramming in a late evening workout while she was watching television by herself or talking on the phone with her boyfriend.

Jennifer eventually confronted me about our lack of time together and let me know how she felt about the status of our friendship. I understood and told her I would do better. And I did, for a little while, then fell back into my isolating ways. In my defense, I had always been a fairly independent kid, never needing anyone to help me get through life. I had learned early on that the ones closest to us often let us down and I relied on no one to make me feel complete. While this is a good quality for survival, it is less so for fostering friendships.

The tension continued to build and Jennifer made a statement by bringing home a kitten one day. She never consulted me about the decision, which brought my own irritation with our relationship into play. The problem I had with the new four-legged roommate was that my boyfriend was very allergic to cats, as in his eyes swell shut and he can't breathe. Clearly, my boyfriend would never be able to come to my apartment again. The wedge between Jennifer and me got noticeably bigger.

One of our last major arguments as roommates happened when Jennifer arrived back in town after going on vacation with her boyfriend's family. She had asked me to water her plants and take care of her cat while she was gone. Normally that wouldn't have been a problem, but it was spring break and my fiancé was back in Omaha for the week. He was helping a friend who owned a lawn and landscape business and was looking forward to making a little extra cash during the break. However, during one of the first days he was at work, they were cleaning gutters and he slipped on a wood-shingled roof. Both feet went out from under him, causing him to fall off the two-story house. Luckily, he was able to grab a tree branch on the way down which slowed his fall, but he still landed with enough force to shatter his wrist.

I spent the next several days at the hospital after work while he recovered from surgery, then helped him get situated at his parents' house. I wanted to be with him as much as I could; Huxley and watering plants were the last things on my mind. My fiancé could have been paralyzed or died, and every second with him was infinitely more precious than before.

I was at work when Jennifer returned home from vacation. I answered the phone and I heard, "What the hell happened while I was gone? My plants are dead and Huxley acts as if he hasn't see anyone all week!" And she was right. I had gone to the apartment to take care of Huxley but it was just long enough for me to shower, eat a quick bite, and scoop out the litter box. I didn't stay to play with him; I did the necessary functions of keeping the cat alive. The plants were overlooked because I didn't even turn on the living room light when I came to the apartment. They were left in the shadows to wither away.

Looking back on it, I can't blame her for her initial reaction because I had failed her so many times before. However, in the moment, my blood was boiling as I explained what happened to my fiancé. I couldn't wait for her to eat her words. There was a long chunk of silence as she absorbed what I had said then eventually asked if he was okay. I don't even remember how we ended the conversation, but that was the day I started packing up my things and migrated to my future in-law's' house.

My fiancé moved back home because he could no longer work at his college job to help pay for his rent and tuition. My relationship with Jennifer became non-existent, and I wasn't surprised when she informed me she was moving out when our lease was up. I technically had already moved out on her but felt the crack in our friendship become a canyon when she revealed she was moving to Denver.

When her moving day came, I was at work but had told her I would leave early to see her off. I took a call that afternoon that I will forever regret. Rather than leave at the agreed time, I had answered a call from a candidate whom I had been trying to get ahold of. I should have let my partner handle the call and I should have left. During my call, I saw my partner answer my other phone line and then mouthed the words, "Your roommate." I nodded and held up my finger as I continued the call. Jennifer, sick of waiting, eventually hung up. I don't even know if I convinced the guy to take the job. I tried calling her back at the apartment but there was no answer. I packed up for the day and left. But in my gut, I knew she was gone.

I arrived to a mostly empty apartment. The only things left were my bedroom furniture, my meager kitchenware, and a pile of bills. And a parting note.

Jennifer explained that she had done most of the cleaning and that I could do the rest, that is, if I bothered to show up. She had also left checks for her portion of our remaining utility bills. At the time, I was angry, blaming her for not understanding the demands of my job and that a lot was riding on that call.

I was a fool. The only thing riding on that call was

our friendship. I hadn't been there for her so many times during that year together, and when she wrote to me a couple of months later, I wasn't surprised when she told me she wasn't going to be in my wedding.

Since then, Jennifer's absence in my life has felt like a chasm I'd never be able to fill. I felt it in my wedding preparations. I felt it on my wedding day. I felt it when I became a mother for the first time as well as the last. Not one of those moments in my life happened without thinking of her. Almost ten years went by before I found the courage to deal with the overwhelming need to make peace with her. I missed her terribly and wanted to show her I could be a better friend. I found her mailing address in our sorority's alumni directory and wrote her a letter.

I apologized for my part in our breakup and expressed my sorrow over our miscommunication, my lack of effort in our friendship, and for taking our time together for granted. Months went by and I never heard back from her. It hurt that she refused to write back but I figured I deserved it.

Why I tried again, I have no idea. The guilt still lingered as I still thought about her quite often and I wanted to know what she was doing, what her life looked like. The pain of our breakup became more acute with each major event in my life, knowing she was out there experiencing her own major life events without me.

I searched for her in our alumni directory again and this time, I found her email address. I told myself I would try one more time.

I told her about the first letter and that I wondered if she had received it. Again, I explained my feelings, apologized, and asked for the chance to rekindle our friendship. This time she responded. She had never received my letter and was actually happy to hear from me. She did her own apologizing for our breakup and that she also wanted to rekindle our friendship. I'll be forever grateful to that little voice in my head that said, *try again*.

Even though we don't talk as often as we'd like, when we do, I feel the gap of time apart closing up with each conversation. I've been blessed to share in the news of both of her pregnancies as well as visit her and her family whenever we travel to Colorado for vacation. While we are both juggling our roles as busy mothers, we make it a point to reach out whenever we can.

While the time apart has left its mark—ten years is hard to ignore—we've done our best to reduce the scars. While luck may not have much to do with our friendship now, I feel very lucky to have her in my life… again.

*Hallie Sawyer is a writer who has been published in* KCParent, SIMPLYkc, *and* HerLife *magazines. She is also a contributor at* Great New Books. *and can also be found at* www.HallieSawyer.com. *She resides in the Kansas City area with her three children and husband.*

# SOMETIMES IT'S YOUR CHILDREN WHO TEACH YOU

---

ALYSON HERZIG

I've never been a person who's had a lot of friends. I kept my circle small.

You see, growing up I switched schools in sixth grade and had a very hard time making any friends in my new school. Other friendships had already been established and I was shy. Add in my gawkiness and it was a recipe for loneliness. I bonded with another girl who was also new to the school that year and we got along wonderfully—but it was just the two of us. We went to different high schools after that, and then when she went away to boarding school we lost touch.

In high school I was too focused on my boyfriend to take the time to cultivate any friendships. I had one close friend and that was it. She hurt my feelings when she started up a sexual relationship with my ex-boyfriend a week after we broke up. I was unable to forgive her, and never blamed him for his part. I should have recognized they were both at fault, but I didn't.

College was more of the same, one close friend—my roommate. But then she pledged a sorority, and I was unable to because I was broke. I was working two jobs to get by and my father was out of work due to health issues. I didn't have the $500 to join. I was heartbroken that I couldn't pledge. I watched all the other girls I knew make new friends and form tight-knit bonds with one another. My roommate and I stayed close, and we lived together for four out of the five years I lived in Pittsburgh, where I attended college. We grew apart when I moved away for a job and she moved across the country.

I basically had no close friendships for the next five or six years. I was busy establishing my career and I fell in love with my husband. It wasn't until after our son was born that I connected with other women. I had a close friendship with another new mom and we spoke daily. Our lives were parallel, and it was nice to have someone to lean on and joke with about all things new mom. But then she moved away, and again I was left alone nursing a void in my heart that had become all too common in my life.

It's strange not having anyone close to confide in or to joke with. But then again, there is no one that can hurt you. I have built up walls throughout my life to avoid being hurt. Initially they were in response to the pain of having a parent that was ill since I was three years old. We (my sisters and I) were not allowed to show sadness, or worry, in our house. We were to accept our father's latest setback and move on: no drama, no tears. We were required to be stoic, or we were chastised. The walls were created out of necessity, out of fear.

This mental compartmentalizing has aided me when friends have betrayed me, or hurt me, or moved on. It has made it possible to exist without friendships. I do not dwell on it; I persevere over it.

By the time I was in my mid-twenties, I accepted that I would have few friends in my life. It never dawned on me that my lack of friendships would have an impact on my children. However, once they were in preschool I began to realize that my kids were missing out on observing models of good friendship. I had never put it together before, but I was newly aware that my own mother never showed us how to be a good friend, and I was following in her footsteps.

I became more cognizant of other women's friendships around me, longing to be invited into the fold. However, my shyness made it difficult to bond with them. I watched from the sidelines as other people's friendships developed and grew, waiting to find someone who had similar interests, appreciated my forwardness, and could lob sarcasm back and forth. I wanted a friend, but you don't just go and pick a friend out at the mall. It's not like getting a new shirt. There has to be a connection, a commonality. Where was I going to find this in my community? My kids went to a conservative religious school, and I have strong liberal feelings and beliefs.

But then it happened. I stayed after school one day to help my daughter's Girl Scout troop plant some flowers. I looked up and there was a mom that I knew I wanted to meet. She was unlike any other person I had met in the ten years we had lived in the area. She was wearing a tank top that showcased her tattoos. Historically, I have found people with tattoos tend to be creative, fun, and open to having a drink or two—all major requirements in friendship for me. I introduced myself, and we immediately hit it off; it was like we were meant to be friends. She had an older boy who was a lot like my son, and we understood each other's difficulties.

Molly and I spent a lot of time together that first summer. Our daughters bonded instantly, and our boys, although a year apart in age, got along well too. Even our husbands liked each other!

Our families spent long weekends together at our cottage, and leaned on each other through tough times and rejoiced in each other's wins.

Our bond was so close that we joked about living in a commune together someday. I felt like I was owed this friendship from life, that finally I had been handed the thing I had been wanting for years.

However, like all of the good friendships before in my life, this one too came to an end. It started to unravel gradually. There were moments when one of us didn't appreciate the other enough, and visa versa. Feelings got hurt, and seeds of anger were planted. It's funny how quickly hostility can grow.

Snide comments were made that were not addressed or resolved. The anger grew, spreading from an isolated incident, snuffing out the good in our bond and replacing it with the bad after three years of closeness.

Promises were made and then broken. Shock and disbelief that someone you cared for so much was not there when you really needed it. And like crabgrass, the anger eventually began taking over the lawn, choking out the lush landscape and replacing it with barren ugliness.

We still crossed paths at our kids' school, but our interactions were icy. Everyone around us knew something was up, but we didn't discuss what had happened. It was too raw, that moment on the phone when we finally ripped into each other over the issues we had. The feelings of anger and hurt, the words that spewed from each of our mouths were painful and unnecessary. Things were dragged up from long ago that would have been better left buried. We both let it all out in one angry and intense conversation.

I hung up the phone and seethed about what was said, I cried about what was lost, and I then did the most immature thing ever—I unfriended her on Facebook. Now, a year later, it makes me laugh, but at the time I felt like she should have no knowledge of my daily life, no interaction with my kids, nothing.

The pull apart was complete. We didn't talk for eight months, and our daughters suffered.

"Mommy," my daughter asked me one day, "will I ever get to see Emelia again, since you and Molly are mad at each other?"

"Of course, honey. Mommy and Molly's relationship has nothing to do with you and Emelia."

But I was wrong. The girls saw each other intermittently. Our issues became a strain on them. I had hoped they would move on, as I always did. But they were too close.

Ultimately, it was my eight-year-old who taught me a life lesson. She asked me, "Why can't you and Molly just be friends like Emelia and I are? Why can't you talk it out and forgive each other?"

I didn't have an answer. At her age friendship is black and white; there is no grey. I tried to explain that there are things in life kids shouldn't worry themselves about, that what was going on between me and Molly was an adult problem.

But in the end she was right. Why couldn't we just forgive each other?

We reconnected after Emelia invited my daughter to her birthday party. We talked for the first time in months. It was awkward and we only spoke for a few minutes, but it was the beginning. I left and, shortly afterward, she sent me a text message. I called her, and we talked for a while. We caught up on what we had both been doing. She had started a new business, and I was excited for her. She had been following my writing; I was surprised but happy to know she still cared enough.

The wall began to come down.

I reached out to Molly a few weeks later. We were both hesitant to relive the hurt that we'd caused one another. We agreed that we both had said things that were wrong, that we both had our feelings trounced, and that we both acted in ways that we shouldn't have. We have also agreed to move forward, because some friends are worth the extra effort.

I am thankful to my daughter for teaching me the power of true friendship. Sometimes life delivers you that perfect person, and through the highs and lows, you need to make an effort to continue to water the garden or it will become filled with weeds.

*Originally from NJ, Alyson now lives in the Midwest but has kept her sarcastic cynical Jersey attitude. You can find her blogging about the many disasters and observations of her life at* TheShitastrophy.com. *Alyson's other works have been published at* Mamapedia.com, WhatTheFlicka.com, InThePowderRoom.com, *and* BonBonBreak.com *and she is a regular contributor to* LeftyPop.com. *Alyson is the co-creator of the anthology,* Surviving Mental Illness with Humor, *which will be available in 2015.*

# LOST AND FOUND AGAIN

LEA GROVER

My older sister nearly missed my wedding. I'd known from the day I got engaged that she probably would, and I only asked her to stand up with me because she'd fly off the handle if I didn't. I also knew that two months later I could call her and apologize. I would make up some excuse and ask if it was okay for another friend to stand in her place. I knew there would be relief in her voice when she said "yes."

I didn't tell her that this friend was the first person I asked, that she already had a dress, and that asking my older sister at all was simply family politics. It had nothing to do with friendship.

My older sister and I hadn't been friends for a long time.

When you're only eighteen months apart, you'd think you would be close. And once upon a time, we were. We laughed together, read awful pulp romance novels in the middle of the night together, practiced makeup together. She teased me mercilessly, tried her hardest to humiliate me in front of her own friends. Of course she did; we competed constantly and I wanted her friends to like me. I wanted to *be* her friend. It's part of what being a little sister is about.

And truly, we were friends.

Even when we were teenagers and her experimentation began to turn towards something harder and darker, we were friends. Sort of.

But our friendship died when I was 16. When she'd wandered back home after totaling the 86′ Nova I thought of as *mine*, after disappearing for three months to hop trains and sleep in squats and use drugs with whomever was offering. When she came back she had on the same clothes as the day she left, her hair had congealed into dreadlocks filled with lice, and she walked through the front door as though nothing had changed. As though she'd never left.

I rode in the back seat as she and a friend took me to some dingy apartment where she was planning to stay, and watched them shoot up using the remnants from the bottom of an old bottle of Diet Coke I handed over from the mess at my feet.

That night, my parents told me the plan to call the cops and have them pick her up on a bench warrant for totaling the car. I volunteered to keep her at home until they arrived. She'd hang out with me, she wouldn't be suspicious, I told them.

*I'm her friend.*

When they dragged her off the street, spitting and cursing at everyone in ear shot, I sat alone in the basement feeling like a monster. Some Judas who sent my own sister to jail. Even if it was for her own good. But she didn't know I was in on it.

From jail they sent her to a clinic, and I was there when she walked through the door. She sat down next to me. "Hey Lea, what's up?"

I tried not to gape at her. "Um, not a lot. How about you?"

"They want to make me go in here. But I'm not going."

"Oh?"

"No, I'm not."

She said it calmly, as a fact. And when two large orderlies simply picked up my 4'11 waif of a sister, she screamed and kicked until she was long out of sight, until I was sure the sound of her was just an echo in the back of my mind. Just my own guilt.

But that was only the beginning. As soon as she was out of the clinic again she was gone, hopping trains, doping up. Soon my sister started fading away completely. She wasn't my friend anymore, she was a stranger. A stranger who came into my house wearing my sister's face and left dirty needles on the bathroom floor. A stranger who threatened to kill herself every other month, and always meant it, who fell asleep behind the wheel of her car and managed not to die when it rolled over. Every time my phone rang I was sure *this had to be it.* This was the call that she was finally dead. That I could stop worrying about it. That I could stop waiting for it to happen.

And then came the fight. In my house, in the middle of the night, in the dead of winter. She told me she knew I thought I was better than her, and I didn't answer.

I didn't answer because she was right, and she was also so wrong.

I did think I was better than she was, but not better than the person I'd known my whole life. Not better than the girl I had idolized, looked up to, wanted to impress with my intellect and talent and enthusiasm every day of our childhood. I wasn't better than that girl.

The person in front of me was an impostor. A lying, stealing, angry, venomous creature who had stolen my sister from me and replaced her with this foul thing.

As she glared at me, I squared my shoulders. I sighed as I looked at her furious, glazed eyes. "Yeah," I said. "I do."

And she walked out. Out of my house with no real coat in the freezing cold. And I didn't follow her. Not because I was a terrible sister. Not because I was a terrible friend. But because I knew it wouldn't do any good. I'd lost her. The heroin had taken her and she was gone.

Five months later I got married. She made it to the wedding, barely. And in a dopey fog she told me, "I thought this was just going to be a really shitty time. You know, the Lea and Mike Show. But you went to a lot of trouble to make sure everyone had a good time, and you did a good job."

And my heart broke a little bit because I knew that every time I would think back to my wedding day, that would be my favorite moment. The moment I caught a glimpse of my sister inside the shell she had become and she told me she was proud of me.

A few years later she got clean.

I avoided her. I was still wracked with guilt about letting her run off in a bleak Chicago winter with nowhere to go. I was still angry about so many years of being let down, still furious with her for all the days I'd sat with our parents while she recovered from an overdose that should have been fatal.

It wasn't until she'd been on methadone for a few years that I really let myself see she was back.

I had lost my friend. One of my best friends. My sister.

And I was lucky, because after a decade I have her again. I can talk with her, joke with her. She comes to visit and we go to lunch, and she plays with her nieces, and she's *happy*.

"I didn't used to want to get old," she told me. "I assumed I'd be dead and I was fine with it. But now I want to get to know them when *they're* old ladies. I want to live long enough to know my nieces then. I want to be part of their lives."

I want to get to know the old lady she'll become someday, too.

*Lea Grover is a writer and toddler-wrangler, living in Chicago. She waxes philosophic about raising interfaith children, marriage after cancer, and vegetarian cooking. Her blog,* Becoming SuperMommy, *won second runner up during in Blogger Idol, and her work has been featured broadly such places as the* Huffington Post, Scary Mommy, The Daily Mail Online, *and her daughters' toy refrigerator door. When she isn't revising her upcoming memoir, she can be found singing opera to her children or smeared to the elbow in Townsend pastels.*

---

# WHAT WE'VE LEARNED

---

# REFLECTIONS: AN INTRODUCTION

STEPHANIE SPRENGER

Friendship is complex, and sometimes the end of one, when it comes, is not so easily contained by the word "breakup." Sometimes friends simply drift away, and sometimes they drift back in. Often, there is no discernible rift to pinpoint, just a natural, albeit disconcerting, parting of ways. As we move from phase to phase of our lives, there are usually casualties; the flux of our ever-changing roles inevitably has an impact on our friendships. In my own life, I've noticed this phenomenon particularly when it comes to old friends—from childhood, high school, or college. Sometimes it's difficult to tell if the friendship has actually ended.

When I reflect on my oldest friendships, the only ones that have survived were marked by a period of years in which we drifted out of each other's lives, established ourselves in new roles, relationships, and locations, and eventually came back together when we were certain we had found our footing. Often, I have criticized myself for an apparent inability to sustain old friendships during periods of transition. Some of my closest friends, the women I swore I could never live without, have vanished from my life for years at a time. And while there may have been initial awkwardness when we reunited, there was never any residual bitterness or blame; we simply accepted that we needed to let go of our relationship while we navigated new waters and reinvented ourselves.

And sometimes, maddeningly, we don't yet have the perspective to see how our relationships are going to play out in the long run. Some friendships that have lapsed are more mysterious, leaving us wondering if we'll find our way back together in the end. For me, there is one friend—my best friend from high school—whose role in my life is still unclear.

***

I loved her fiercely, as only a chemically-imbalanced adolescent could. We held hands in the hallway, wrote long notes to one another during classes, and laughed to the point of tears at private jokes, the hilarity of which was undoubtedly questionable and existed for reasons I can no longer recall. I craved her presence, and she made me feel more worthwhile than I suspected I was—more talented, more attractive, wittier, and more interesting. She was beautiful, and intelligent, and self-assured. Her friendship made me feel like I too was all of those things, and just being together made me feel there was a place I belonged.

We sang together in choir, shared a voice teacher, and cemented our relationship during an elite, audition-only Honors Choir camp for high school upperclassman. We bonded in the way that teenagers do during intense periods of co-habitation, liberated from the restrictions of our families and their expectations. Her name was

Elizabeth. We were similarly matched in terms of musical talent and achievement, but there was just enough difference between us to disengage any competitiveness—she played in the orchestra, I played in the marching band. We both had serious boyfriends—hers older, mine younger—and our friendship lacked any petty jealousy or insecurity. I believe it was our loyalty and affection for one another that superseded any inclination to succumb to rivalry.

When we were seventeen, Elizabeth and I competed in a rigorous state vocal competition. When we arrived at the performance hall with our families and voice teacher, we were shocked to discover that we were the only two competitors in our category. Although the judges had the option of declaring "no winner" if they determined that neither of us performed well enough to earn the title, for the first time, we would be direct rivals. At the end of the performance, I received the first-place award and passage into the divisional level of competition; Elizabeth was awarded an honorable mention. After receiving the judges' scores, Elizabeth and I stood in the hallway, wrapped our arms around each other and sobbed. To this day, that moment is what I recall most vividly: not winning first place, but the beauty of a friendship that transcended bitterness and somehow encapsulated both the grief of disappointment and the joy of victory. For we shared both.

I felt more deeply bonded to Elizabeth than any other friend I had known—we had exchanged words confirming our commitment to one another, naming it with the most coveted of teenage superlatives—and I was certain our connection would survive the transition to college. Of course, my adolescent naïveté didn't make room for the possibility that our respective evolutions might interfere with our friendship. When we were first reunited after several months—which seemed, in that intense first year of college, like years—I felt a chill in her presence. We were not what we once were. We did not belong to one another anymore. I had recently ended my relationship with my high school boyfriend, another connection I was certain could survive anything, and I had the discomfiting sensation that I didn't belong to anything or anyone—maybe not even myself.

It was that year of my life where the pendulum swung so far from one side to the other that I felt like a whiplash victim. There was no temperance in that turbulent stage of late adolescence, no wisdom to moderate change by small degrees. It was all or nothing for me. I didn't go in for a subtle makeover—I simply shed my skin. Lacking in life experience, neither of us chose to expend the effort it would take to bridge the gap between who we were before and who we had become. We simply gave up and drifted apart.

Ten years later, when our high school reunion rolled around, we excitedly emailed and agreed to meet there. Even after years without contact, there was no awkwardness or animosity, only laughter and enthusiasm as Elizabeth patted my pregnant belly and I chatted amiably with her new boyfriend. Our palpable connection that evening renewed my certainty in the bond between us, although we would not see each other again for over five years.

When I was pregnant with my second daughter, Elizabeth's brother moved to my city. We shared an exhilarating dinner with both of our extended families one Easter weekend, and I knew we'd see each other again when Elizabeth returned to visit her brother at Christmas. I was delighted at the prospect of her regular presence in my life.

When she came the following December, my new baby was nearly three months old, and we planned another dinner. We met at a trendy restaurant downtown, and it became clear within the first five minutes that our meal was not going to be the relaxing, enjoyable, glee-filled reunion that I had hoped for. I'm not sure why this came as such a shock; it certainly wasn't my first time attempting to dine in public with my two young children. I knew there would be rushing, spilling, crying, breastfeeding, complaining, and writhing. What I didn't expect was the fact that I would feel so uncomfortable.

As I sat distractedly nursing my baby, I listened to my childless companions, Elizabeth and both of our brothers, discussing politics and their burgeoning careers. My cheeks flushed with the realization that I had nothing to contribute to the conversation. I felt very much out of place. The admiration and pride I'd felt at Elizabeth's accomplishments and intelligence were now darkened by the one emotion I had never before experienced in our friendship: envy. Envy, accompanied by its graceless companion, self-doubt.

Parenthood was now the chasm that separated us. Was it irreparable? I felt as though I had let Elizabeth down. I felt like she expected more from me—more witticisms, more insights, more *anything* than what I was able to give as the mother of a newborn. For me, that night was the apex of the disquieting experience that occurs when two people do not have the common circumstances to unite them despite shared history and years of emotional intimacy.

It has been over two years since our last meeting, and I wonder if Elizabeth has also sensed the creeping void or if it was all in my head. I have kept up with her life on Facebook. But whenever she shares a link referencing a relevant topic or breaking news story, I feel that familiar surge of discomfort with the juxtaposition of my own status updates—primarily photos of my children or funny family stories. Elizabeth occasionally leaves an endearing or supportive comment on my posts, which gives me pause. Does the issue have more to do with my own insecurity and envy? I look through the photos she shares of her trips—she frequently travels internationally for work—and I wonder if she has been to Colorado in the past few years and hasn't gotten in touch. I suspect she has.

The next time I see Elizabeth, I will have emerged from the self-sacrificing, sleep-deprived haze of parenting a very young child. Someday, it will matter less which career and family paths we have each pursued. The years I spent growing and feeding babies, the same years she spent in graduate school, traveling the world, and climbing her professional ladder, will not be such an obstacle to our friendship. We will have shed a hundred skins by then and we will have the wisdom that comes with those extra years on Earth. I do not believe that our story has ended; when I think of Elizabeth and our hypothetical future reunions, I see a friendship that is still relevant, a connection that mattered deeply to two teenage girls, and matters still.

***

Without the benefit of hindsight, it's hard to predict which friendships will stand the test of time. The essays in this final section of the book reflect themes of ambiguity and uncertainty, of hard work and difficult choices, of exploring seasons of loss and appreciating friendships that have been salvaged. As the writers expose some of the uncomfortable decisions they have made and confess to the roles they have themselves played in the collapse of their relationships, each sheds a unique light on the messy, painful, and sometimes dark side of friendship. Together they remind us that, although we don't always discuss it, women's friendships are often imbued with complexity and are very rarely black and white.

# A SEASON OF LOSS

KATIE SLUITER

I can only remember three times in my 36 years when I have fought with friends. Only one of those times ended in a "break" in the friendship, but we grew up, forgot what it was about (a guy), and moved on.

You see, you have to have friends to break up with them.

It's not that I don't have any friends, but as I get older, I find it's harder and harder to keep friends.

I don't mean that I get involved in drama or fights or misunderstandings and have a hard time holding on to friends. In order for fall-outs to happen, I would actually have to see or speak with my friends. I would have to be with my friends.

It's not that I hate my friends either. I am not purposefully ignoring them or avoiding them. In fact, I will see a friend, we will have a great time, I will blink and six months will go by before I realize I haven't communicated with her other than liking a few Facebook statuses or pictures.

This happens because of the season my life is in right now: Friend Loss.

I spent my teen years and my early twenties in a season called Friend Collection, at which I completely excelled. I turned away no one. In high school I hung out with people who were older, younger, more popular, less popular, athletes, and band kids. In college I went to parties in basements and in frat houses. I said yes to checking out jam bands and going to the dollar movies. I surrounded myself with people who made me laugh.

By my mid-twenties I was in a new season: Friend Maintenance. I tried to keep up with everyone. I emailed and sent cards. We had graduated from college by this point and many of us had moved away from each other. I went on spontaneous road trips to see buddies who were now spread over the state, rather than just down the road.

Even after my husband, Cortney, and I were married, we continued to try to fit in trips and phone calls and weekly communication with our closest friends. But though we had not yet had our first child, we still began to see the first signs of the Friend Loss season.

Friend Loss is very much like winter in that it sneaks in disguised as beauty before the sub-zero temperatures keep us inside for weeks. Just as the leaves slowly show hints of change, Friend Loss begins as a few missed texts or good intentions turned calls never made. Just as the cold creeps in at night first before chilling the day, Friend Loss seems like Friend Postponement—it feels like you are busy right now, but will have time later.

After giving birth to my son, Eddie, I was diagnosed with postpartum depression and anxiety. But I had already sped up the season of Friend Loss by isolating myself because of depression, anxiety, rage, and paranoia.

I said hurtful things in an attempt to thwart the wounds I was sure would come as a result of the plots against me.

Like a sharp cold snap that kills any of the remaining vegetation in my garden, my paranoia and anxiety manifested in the form of a rage that killed many of my remaining friendships. By the time Eddie was a toddler, only the heartiest plants in my yard were still going strong. Only a few friends still stuck around no matter what hell my brain was putting me through.

And then I was pregnant again. When Charlie was born, I had a better grip on this new season in my life, but there wasn't any going back. The season marched on as my life filled first with children, then with work opportunities. When free time was available, I mostly chose my husband and children rather than reaching out to my friends.

Before children, when I got out of work I could go to the gym, run errands, get dinner with a friend, or figure out dinner with my husband whenever we got hungry. Now our lives have become more structured with daycare pick-up, a set dinner time, and bath/bed-time routines. There just isn't room in my week for anything outside of work and family. The weekends are not much different. Because the kids are in daycare more than forty hours a week, weekends are sacred to us. We don't want to rush them off to a sitter, so if it isn't a family invite, we don't go.

When you don't put time into something, it dies. Because we chose strict nap schedules, swim lessons, and Sunday school, we have to say "no" to happy hour, spontaneous lunch dates, and Girls Night Out.

With an almost-five-year-old and an almost-two-year-old and thoughts of adding to our family again, I realize that the colorful beauty that initiated this season is gone. The leaves have fallen and have left bare branches where many friends once hung. There are a few friends who, like evergreen trees, remain regardless of the season in my life.

But it's hard to cultivate new friendships in this season.

My planner is full, my house is busy, and there are just so many hours in a day. While I feel utterly unfriendable, I know this is all mostly by my own choice.

I chose this life of mine when I said, "I do" to Cortney on that warm June day in 2005. I said "yes" to filling my days and weekends with dinosaur chicken nuggets rather than fruity martinis when I smiled at that positive pregnancy test after a homecoming football game in 2008.

While winter tends to feel like the end of life, we know that it is not. Spring and rebirth will come. I'm starting to see that Friend Loss is that way too.

I'm already noticing some of my friends with kids older than mine are entering a season of Deep Friendships. They are reconnecting with old friends and making new friends. They are spending quality time and supporting each other.

It's heartening to see, but I am not there yet.

I am still in the frozen season of Friend Loss.

It is painful to hear cold, howling wind where once there was a lively conversation.

It is hurtful to feel the sting of the cold silence where once there were texts and emails.

It is depressing to look at the almost thousand Facebook "friends" I have knowing I can count on one hand how many of those are truly still my friends.

But this is my season. This is the life I have chosen. It is lonely at times, but there is comfort in knowing it is but a season, and will pass.

*Katie Sluiter (pronounced Sly-ter) lives in Zeeland, Michigan. She is a wife, mom, teacher and writer who holds a Master's Degree in English Education and works as a junior high school English instructor, adjunct college English instructor, and an advocate for the Common Core State Standards with the Michigan Education Association. Her writing has been featured on* Borderless News and Views, BonBon Break, *the Imagine Toys blog, and* BlogHer. *She was interviewed for* TODAY MOMS *in 2013. She is also a contributing author to the book* Three Minus One: Stories of Parents' Love and Loss *(2014).*

# CONFESSIONS OF A SERIAL FRIENDSHIP ABANDONER

GALIT BREEN

This story begins in the only place that it can—at the very end. My friendship breakup affected my entire family, was prolonged, painful—and utterly necessary.

Because after the breakup and the mourning and the questioning and the mourning and the anger and then even more mourning, I became a better person and a much better friend.

The lessons learned from this friendship breakup were all mine. I gleaned the one trait that I absolutely had to change in order to become the kind of friend that I wanted to be, and that I expected of others.

I was a stubborn student and this lesson was hard learned.

"The friendship clearly wasn't working for either one of us," was my mantra. I repeated it to my husband every time the topic of my friendship breakup arose, which was, admittedly, annoyingly often. For a very long time, he was the only person I talked to about it. The intimacy required to share something so personal was too much for me, so he was my sounding board, my willing shoulder to lean on, and my reluctant but proficient armchair analysis-provider.

We would sit in the center of our bed like our three children often do. Our room large, but our space within it small. Our toes touching, our voices whispering, mine often skating the line between anger and tears. I would ask what he thought had happened, how he thought their family was doing, if he thought we would ever find our way back to each other.

The answers he gave me were simple and unwavering: *We didn't trust each other. Well, I hope.* And *probably not.*

His words were often not what I wanted to hear, but their edges softened the more times he said them.

The relationship my friend and I had was threaded with our husbands and our children. It was based on same professions, similar politics, the desire to meld with another family, to be chosen for holidays and birthdays and vacations and spontaneous weeknight dinners and weekend coffees and morning walks.

The problem was that at the time I didn't trust, anyone really, enough to let them in that deeply. I wanted that kind of friendship, without the vulnerability required to have it. I was a serial friendship abandoner for this exact reason.

When things got hard or tricky or uncomfortable, I left. I answered phone calls with silence, plans with cancellations, and chance meetings with coldness. What I wanted to avoid was discomfort first, and the risk of rejection second.

I viewed friendships as fragile and just a step away from ruin. So I beat hurt to the punch and did the dirty (abandoning) deed before I could be the one who was abandoned.

So when my friend did something I didn't like—I pulled away from her. And when I missed her, and when my family missed hers, I tried to bury my hurt and dive back into our friendship, only to repeat the cycle.

This was, of course, unbearably unfair of me.

Our story ended many years ago. And the nights of trying to unravel what had happened, and my role in it, ended a few years after that. Once that path was cleared, it took two tries—with two friends—to learn what I needed to from my friendship breakup.

The first time I handled it poorly, relying on my old go-tos of avoidance and abandonment. But what was different was that I could immediately see the mistake I was making. And the second time, as I was getting good and ready to follow my usual marching orders, I was told exactly what I needed to hear.

So what's my big secret? What are the cold hard words I needed to hear and truly listen to? What one change did I need to make to break my viscous abandoning cycle?

I needed to learn how to trust in the strength of friendships and of my own friendability.

Here's how I learned that.

I went to a writing conference with a friend. She surprised me with some of her actions while we were there and I had a hard time reconciling who she was there with who she was here. My (unfortunate) gut reaction was to pull away. To spend less time together. To avoid the hard *What the heck happened?* conversation. But she didn't let me do any of these things.

She addressed everything from my observations at the conference to my behavior when we got back home head-on. I was honest with my discomfort in having the conversation, and here's what she told me.

Friendships sometimes feel uncomfortable.

Discomfort doesn't weaken. In fact, when handled correctly, it strengthens.

Because still being "in it" after the discomfort will mean knowing that our friendship isn't delicate or fragile, that it's not going to break because of a problem.

Her words were as simple as that, and just as hard to hear as my husband's were all those times from the center of the big bed.

But they gave me the freedom to be more human in my friendships. To change my expectations. To forgive more freely. To realize that there isn't a chance of agreeing with absolutely everything that a friend does. But that this isn't necessary anyway.

That stepping into discomfort and unpredictability and lack of control is part of friendship.

Today I'd like to say that I sit with discomfort easily. But I won't lie to you. I have to consciously remind myself to step into uncomfortable conversations. To be direct about what I want and don't want and to be completely okay with the possible outcomes—a mutual, fair drift or a stronger bond, trust, and friendship.

Many, many years later, my friendship breakup still pops into my mind regularly. I have fond memories of our families' time together and I (truly) hope she's well. I've thought—so very many times—of reaching out to her. But I realize that as much as my story has changed, hers probably has, too, and the years and distance and memories between us are at a resting spot just as they are. I'm grateful for both the friendship we had and the lesson I learned from our breakup.

*On any given day Galit Breen can be found juggling three kids, one husband, one puggle, and her laptop. Galit has had essays published in several anthologies, is the editor of* Pens and Paint, *a series anthology of children's poetry and artwork, and co-directs* Listen to Your Mother, Twin Cities. *Galit is a freelance writer for* Everyday Family, Mamalode Magazine, SheKnows's *allParenting,* Soleil Moon Frye's Moonfrye, and The Huffington Post *blog. Galit blogs at* These Little Waves *and may or may not work for dark chocolate.*

# FRENEMIES

LINDA WOLFF

"With friends like these, who needs enemies?"—English proverb.

I've learned a few things in my many days on this earth. One that stands out the most is: if someone or something seems too good to be true, it probably is.

I wasn't always so cynical. I was always one to make fast friends—like puppies in a dog park. The spark of a connection, shared interests or circumstances, and reciprocated warmth, meant we became super close, super fast. I fell into friendships quickly, like love, and I fell a lot in my younger years.

The friendship breakups I have experienced were from a betrayal of some sort or a misunderstanding. Some of the most painful breakups happened during my childhood, when I couldn't fully understand the complexity of people or situations. The friend that moved on in her 20s and 30s because our lives were on totally different paths didn't hurt nearly as much as the one who dumped me in junior high and moved on, without explanation, to a new best friend, or, even worse, a mutual best friend.

Those early friendships were the hardest to let go. The ones we built as we were in the throes of our teenage years, as we were growing and changing and turning into young adults. When we were pulling away from our parents and bonding more with our friends from rebellion or necessity or both. When we made our friendship bracelets and promised we would be "Best Friends Forever".

I think what was most shocking was the feeling of betrayal, which felt completely different from the type of betrayal from a lover. I considered my female friends to be sisters. Naively, I didn't think a breakup could happen. A betrayal from one of my best girl friends went deeper than any man's cheatin' heart (or body part). We were supposed to have each other's backs, right? Until one tries to steal your boyfriend. (Ahem, you know who you are. And, no, I haven't forgiven you.)

What made matters more difficult was that I married several years before the rest of my friends, some of which were still unattached at the time of my wedding. My betrothal must have seemed like I was taking a rocket ship to another planet and leaving them behind. It was at a time when I was the only one of my friends to be engaged or even remotely close to marriage, so I began to feel like an outsider amongst my peers.

Some of the new friendships I made during this time were with other "couple" friends. They were not my best decisions and felt transient after a while. I guess we were all trying to find some normalcy and new sense of belonging as we were beginning our lives as couples and bringing tiny little people into the world.

***

Here are a few types of friends that slipped away or that I felt the need to distance myself from:

The one who wouldn't speak to me for days because she always had to win at EVERYTHING.

The one who cut off all her friends when she moved, literally, over the hill, and we were no longer geographically convenient.

The one who was only happy when she was making someone feel bad.

The one who tried to move into my friendships and then leave me out of their social plans.

The one who always lied. About everything!

The one who wanted to turn the entire pregnancy process into a competition (she tried this with our weddings, too): who would be first to conceive, have the first boy, gain the least weight and then lose it.

The one who wanted to know my every move and every thought—and with the right amount of wine would learn it—yet shared nothing of herself.

The one who gossiped about everyone, and probably gossiped about me the moment I walked away.

To them I am grateful for the lessons learned and say a hearty, "Good riddance!"

***

What makes us choose the friends we do, or do we allow them to choose us? Are they a mirror of our first female relationships with our moms and sisters?

The beauty of getting older is being able to sniff out the agendas and see who is real and who is not. I now take my "fast friends" slowly and listen to my gut. I've learned to take time in my friendships, in my judgments, in many things that should be savored. I'm much more careful now, because I finally understand that there is a big difference between an acquaintance and a friend.

No relationship is perfect, but I have weeded out the ones that have made me feel bad or have felt one-sided. I put time and energy and my heart into relationships that feed me, and I give back to those freely in return. They're mutual platonic love affairs that I deeply cherish, and they have enriched my life immeasurably. And like the relationships with my family, I pray they live forever.

Loyalty, honesty, and kindness are the most important qualities of a friend to me. If they're funny too, then I've hit the jackpot. Over the years I have established a nice group of friends. I have eating buddies, shopping buddies, exercise buddies, and writing buddies. Friends who can keep a secret, friends who cannot, friends to cry with and pour out my heart, and friends with whom I can just shoot the breeze or count on for a good laugh. When I'm really lucky, I have many of those qualities in one person. They all have a place in my heart and my life is better for it.

*Linda Wolff lives in Los Angeles with her husband, and parents two grown children from afar as they pursue higher education. She keeps her fingers crossed that one day they will both move back or she will have to get a puppy. Linda writes the blog* Carpool Goddess, *proof that midlife, motherhood, and the empty nest aren't so scary. Her pieces are as humorous as they are informative. Share in her adventures as she blazes the trail from the teen years to college to empty nest. Linda was recently published in the humor anthology* Not Your Mother's Book On Being A Mom, *and is a frequent contributor on*

Huffington Post, Scary Mommy, Erma Bombecks Writers' Workshop, *and* Felicity Huffman's What The Flicka.

# WHO DOES THAT?

---

MEREDITH NAPOLITANO

Point A: Best friends.

Point B: No contact.

How do you get from here to there?

Most women who have "broken up" with their best friends can cite a big reason why. A major fight. An act of betrayal. A defining moment where the relationship is irrevocably damaged and can't be repaired.

Or maybe you never "broke up," but your relationship did a slow fade. Someone moved away, and the geographical distance was just too much. Lives grew in different directions until the common ground was so narrow it couldn't sustain you. You might stay on the Christmas card list, you might stay on her list of Facebook friends, but if you were having a Girl's Night, she wouldn't make the cut anymore.

I've experienced both the defining moment breakup and the slow fade with many of the friends I've had during my lifetime. In both cases, you get over it. You might grieve, you might look back and feel wistful, but at least you have a sense of closure. The relationship had a definitive end. Something you can give as a reason for that end.

But what if your ending was…silence? Not a defining moment. Not a slow fade. No big argument. No gradual decrease in phone conversations and nights out. One day, you were friends, the next, there was silence.

*** 

My best friend, from the time I was in 4th grade through college, was Janie.

It was a friendship that seemed to endure despite any circumstance. We didn't attend the same elementary or middle school, we didn't live within walking distance of each other, we didn't take dance together or see each other at Girl Scouts. We did a summer youth theater camp together, and made our friendship last.

We were best friends through all those defining girl moments. We shared our Caboodles and tried on makeup together. I was insanely jealous that she had her own phone *and* phone number. She was an only child and seemed to be the beneficiary of extraordinary attention and fortune. She loved my kid-friendly neighborhood and the opportunity to join me in bossing my little sister around.

She was a gifted piano player and I loved to sing. We would sit in her mom's music room and she'd play while I sang and she harmonized while accompanying me. Our voices blended seamlessly. We both played the clarinet, and although she was by far the superior player, it was another connection that we shared.

In high school, we adored the fact that we were finally in the same school. We started to develop different interests, but we stayed close. She had many platonic guy friends and loved "guy" activities like Dungeons and Dragons. I started expanding my theater interests, performing in shows all over the state. Yet we came together and helped each other.

At high school graduation, we, along with a third friend, shared the honor of singing the National Anthem (usually a solo) by performing an a cappella trio her mother had arranged.

We didn't go to college together. She spent a semester at music school before determining that it wasn't for her, and moved back home to figure things out. While I was getting my degree in music education, she was working, taking classes locally, meeting her first husband. We talked, we emailed, we still made the effort.

I was a bridesmaid in her wedding.

I'd just started dating my (now) husband, and although the two of them didn't hit it off the way I thought they would, they both seemed to respect the other's relationship with me. He was my date for her wedding, dropping me off to get ready at her house and shuffling my bags around as I performed my wedding party duties.

As she settled into married life, and I started my job, we continued to drift, but we also worked at maintaining our friendship. She was happy for me when my boyfriend and I announced our engagement. She offered me advice when I was planning my wedding. That year she also saved me by accompanying my children's choir when I was working at a new school. It was my first children's choir and I was lost in the stress of all those "other" aspects. I didn't know how to find a good accompanist, how to be in charge. She helped me. She encouraged me when my supervisor told me he expected my first concert to be a failure. When it snowed the day of my dress rehearsal and horrible traffic kept me from getting to school on time, she was there, warming up my choir, getting them ready when I couldn't.

When that concert was a success, despite my supervisor's prediction, we went out for drinks and mock toasted him and his negativity. And I sighed with relief that she'd be with me for the next one.

But she wasn't.

My wedding was approaching, and she wasn't one of my bridesmaids. I talked to her about it when I'd made that final decision. My husband has close friends, but only a few he wanted in the wedding. My core group in college was made up of four girls who would be included. My sister. His brother. And that was it. She totally understood. At least I thought so.

Then she didn't show up to my bridal shower. No note. No call. No word.

She didn't ever show up again.

She didn't reply to my phone calls or emails about the concert. Nothing.

I worried about her. She'd had some issues with pregnancy and miscarriage, and I wondered if something was really wrong. I sent notes. I left voicemails.

A few weeks before the wedding, I wasn't worried. I was hurt. I wondered if I'd done something wrong. Was she truly offended she wasn't a bridesmaid? Did she think I was taking advantage of her with my choir? Was I not being supportive enough through her pregnancy issues?

I stopped calling.

I stopped emailing.

And I stared at that name on my wedding guest list—no confirmation, no denial.

A couple of weeks before the wedding, when the RSVP

date had long passed, I made my sister email her, playing dumb, "just checking" on those last few invites! Hoping hers hadn't been lost! Meredith really wanted her there for the special day!

She replied to my sister. She'd be there for the ceremony. Not the reception. No details, but she was alive! I sent her a follow up (playing dumb), saying I couldn't wait to see her in the church.

No response.

And was she there on my wedding day?

No.

For the next two years, I sent her a Christmas card. She got a picture of our new house.

But I never heard from her again. And after the second year, I didn't keep her on my card list. I took the hint. I gave up.

We're not Facebook friends, but we have so many friends in common that I've gotten glimpses of her life. I know she's an organist and choir director, just like her mom was. I know she's not married to the same guy. I know she hasn't had any children.

But that best friend from childhood, wrapped up in so many childhood memories is gone. With no closure.

Who *does* that?

Well, I did.

\*\*\*

Lucy and I met when we were temping at an office during a holiday break from college. We both loved books, we got along well, and it wasn't long before we were emailing, calling, and getting together with the boyfriends and becoming a cozy foursome. The guys got along well, we got along well, and they were another *couple* we could hang out with.

Was she in my wedding? Nope, but she was there for me smiling when Janie wasn't.

She and her boyfriend bought a house within walking distance from my apartment. After work, we'd get together for walks. At least once every weekend, we'd be with them at a restaurant, a bar, a mall, a mini golf course.

The thing was, there was a lot of damage under the surface of a great friendship. She and her boyfriend seemed to have a terrible relationship, that she clung on to while he was outwardly nasty to her, and our couple dates became more and more uncomfortable. She was a button pusher—deliberately baiting my husband on issues she knew he'd argue with her about. He moved from being mildly annoyed with her to being visibly irritated with her personality.

She would call me at school while I was teaching, simply because she was bored at her desk. If I forgot to turn my ringer off, that meant an embarrassing moment of being caught with my cell phone on with a class of eight year olds waiting for me to dig it out of my purse and deny the call. She'd email four or five times a day, wondering why I couldn't respond right away.

She used her job as a disability insurance office worker to look up people she knew and see if they were in the system (what seems to be a pretty serious privacy violation). When she found that my husband had once been injured during a college job, she crowed with happiness and brought it up at our next dinner.

My husband thought that was the last straw, and we decided to back off our friendship. They'd become a couple that we weren't having fun with. I was annoyed when the phone rang. He was sick of hearing her boyfriend rant about moving her out of the house because he couldn't stand her, and then turn around and take her on vacation. We were starting to divide up into "the guys" and "the girls", and I resented being stuck with her when I wanted to relax with friends and my husband.

We were going to do the slow fade.

We planned on taking longer to return calls, limiting our availability on weekends, finding other friends. By that point, we had moved into our house and had the excuse of no longer living a convenient block away, so everything was set for a slow fade out.

Then they pinned us down for a dinner, almost immediately after we'd begun to back off. Thinking we were on the verge of becoming "part-time" friends, we were less annoyed, and we were happy to have a night out. Knowing that they weren't our only option anymore, we began to relax and enjoy ourselves.

Then they dropped the bomb that they were engaged and asked us to be in their wedding party—to be a full *fifty percent* wedding party.

Cue awkward looks.

How do you tell two people a flat out *no?* How do you tell them you think they have the least healthy relationship you've ever seen and you can't imagine them making it through a wedding? How can you slowly fade from someone's life if they've told you that you are *half the people they are asking to be in the wedding party?*

Awkward, awkward, horribly awkward. I don't remember exactly how we responded, but I know we didn't say no.

On the drive home we started talking about what to do and how to handle it. Should my husband take her boyfriend out and give it to him straight? Should I try to dig in and find out how they got to this point?

We felt trapped. Trapped in a relationship that we didn't want to be in. Resigned to over a year of faking it, acting like their best friends. We spent that night weighing our options and feeling like horrible people.

So we cut them out.

We didn't answer calls. We didn't reply to emails. We didn't make contact. We made a deal with each other that we would stay strong.

One morning I sat at my desk in tears as an email from her came in, imploring me to answer, wondering why our friendship had ended. Begging me to call her back.

I was a horrible, *horrible* person.

After a week or so, the calls stopped.

The emails stopped.

And just like that, the friendship was over.

I'd done what had hurt me so badly, what I had just managed to get over. I was deliberately putting someone through what I had hated having done to me.

***

I now had an idea of why Janie did what she did. As we grew apart, she began to feel our friendship was forced. When I didn't ask her to be in my wedding, she had confirmation that we were no longer the best friends we'd once been. And one day, she decided that dragging out a friendship was more damaging to her than just cutting me out. She didn't want to have a major confrontation where we were forced to say hurtful things to each other. She didn't want to fake it anymore. She couldn't sit at my wedding, pretending to be happy for me, when she felt nothing but hurt.

So she walked away.

When Lucy asked me to be the one girl she could count on, I couldn't take the pressure of faking a friendship at that level. In general, I think I'm a nice person, I'm a giver. I knew that I would sacrifice my own happiness to keep this false friendship up. I didn't want to have a major confrontation with her where I told her that I didn't like the person she had turned into, and I thought she was making a horrible mistake by getting married to someone who seemed to not like her at all.

So I walked away.

More than other friendship endings, these are the two that have stuck with me.

Cutting someone out, shutting and locking the door with nothing but silence seems cruel. It felt cruel when Janie did it to me. It felt cruel when I did it to Lucy.

I remember wanting to fight with Janie. I yearned to fight for our friendship. I wanted her to say those things that she refused to say. Tell me I'm a bad friend. Tell me that I did wrong. A slap of accusation would surely hurt less than the slow infection of doubt and guilt that I was feeling. Maybe the friendship would have been over, but I'd *know*.

But I remember *not* wanting to fight with Lucy. I didn't want to hurt her with accusations and words. I felt that it would be better in the long run if I just disappeared. She could move on and blame me.

My break up with Lucy finally let me understand what Janie was going through.

Was it the best choice? I don't know. I know that I don't talk about these relationships. I edit life stories so these women are no longer a factor because I don't like having to explain their presence and why it is no longer something I enjoy remembering. I know that I'm ashamed that I was both someone who needed to be cut, and someone who, having experienced that pain, cut someone else.

But I also know that I'm a better friend now thanks to these two relationships. And I hope, sincerely, that both of them feel like they are a better friend after me.

*Meredith Napolitano is a former music teacher and choir director who made the move to stay-at-home mom two years ago. Meredith began writing shortly after this transition, initially as a way to continue having "adult conversations" without bombarding her friends constantly with her daily anecdotes, and slowly making her way into the freelance writing and blogging world. Meredith shares her daily anecdotes of raising two toddler girls, along with reflections about parenting and family, silly stories and moments that have become memories. Most of all, she focuses on writing about the balance between her two roles, "Meredith" and "Mommy". Her writing has been featured on many different sites including* Huffington Post, iVillage, Circle of Moms, *and* Scary Mommy. *Meredith was recently in the best-selling anthology* I Just Want to Be Alone, *where she overshared a funny story about the man in her house full of girls, and will also have an essay appearing in* Motherhood: May Cause Drowsiness, *releasing later this fall. When she's not fulfilling her role as chauffeur, housekeeper, cook, and teacher, she's connecting with moms on social media and writing for her site, "From Meredith to Mommy".*

# INTIMACY, VULNERABILITY, AND HUMILITY

VICKY WILLENBERG

It took six months sharing a shoebox apartment for my husband and I to have our first fight. As I stormed out of the apartment and climbed into my tiny two-door Nissan Sentra, in tears and armed with righteous indignation, my heart was heavy and my mind was racing. I was not naïve enough to think we'd breeze through marriage without a bump in the road. However, knowing that disagreements were inevitable and actually experiencing one were two very different things. The idea that intimacy creates vulnerability, yet provides an opportunity for a stronger relationship, was something I had yet to understand.

As I drove the dark streets of San Diego, processing all the feelings tumbling through my mind (and secretly hoping he was at home feeling guilty and worried about me), I remember feeling so betrayed. This man that I pledged my life to, to whom I bared my soul, my fears and dreams, clearly did not understand me. No matter the issues that lead to this inaugural battle, the crux of it—in my mind— was that my husband did not *know* me. If he had, he would have *seen* where I was coming from and even better, he would have *expected* my response. For the first time in our marriage, I considered the possibility that I married the wrong person. Because surely "The Right Person" would have *just known.* I could finally see why so many people got divorced.

Slowly but surely, the anger began to fade and my mind quieted. Rational thought began to penetrate my brain and brought the vicious cycle of thoughts to a halt. Anger was replaced by a new sensation—shame. Although my frustration and anger might have been justified, it was fueled by my self-centered thinking. It was all about the ways in which I had been wronged, not taking into account any of my own responsibility.

In that moment, I knew that the intimacy that had created my vulnerability also brought with it the opportunity for humility. It was time to cut the dramatics and head home, talk it out and recognize my role in the situation. Acknowledging my unspoken expectations and admitting my assumption that he should just "know me," which translates to "read my mind," was not going to be easy. But if intimacy with my husband was going to be restored and I was ever going to feel safe with the level of vulnerability that comes with a meaningful relationship, jumping ship was not an option. It was time to have the hard conversation.

I would like to say this was a turning point in all my relationships. I wish I could say with confidence that the intimacy-vulnerability-humility pattern came easy from that day forward. Unfortunately, I seem to be a slow learner.

There are few relationships as significant and intimate

as the one between a husband and wife. However, one relationship that is equally intimate and meaningful as the marriage bond is the friendship forged on the battlefield of motherhood. If vulnerability and authenticity breed intimacy, then there's no better stage for that to happen than motherhood. And just as a strained marriage can leave you heartbroken, a friendship balancing on a precipice can be equally painful.

At the age of 39 I sat in my car steeped in hurt, anger and betrayal just as I had as a newlywed at the tender age of 25. There was no driving off into the night this time—I'd grown up a little bit, I guess. But again I was left feeling exposed and vulnerable because a close friendship had fallen short of my expectations. For years our relationship had been so easy, effortless. A comradeship was naturally formed as our paths ran parallel because of our circumstances. School-aged children and husbands working long hours, first homes and new cars, juggling part-time jobs and household responsibilities. "To Do's" were coordinated and our bond grew stronger through hours cruising the aisles of Target with kids in tow, coffee in hand.

But life's paths don't run straight. They twist and turn. They veer left and sometimes disappear around an unseen bend. And the friendship that was once so effortless suddenly took a lot of effort. We suddenly had to be intentional about something that once flowed as naturally as breathing. Worse yet, it came at a time when we had fewer hours to give due to more demands on our time. Schedules no longer coordinated. The miles easily traversed with kids happily tucked in car seats now seemed too difficult to navigate between school and football practice and laundry and homework.

The silence between phone calls stretched farther and the quick texts to "check in" and "touch base" became shorter. There just wasn't time. My path was going left and hers was going right. We'd gone from parallel to perpendicular, heading in two different directions. And as the weight of life's responsibilities grew heavier and heavier, the raft of friendship that once kept me afloat was nowhere to be found and I was drowning. I felt raw and vulnerable, misunderstood and unknown- just as I had as a young married woman.

At this point in my life I had seen countless relationships fall apart—both marital and platonic. Sometimes it was a natural progression of lives changing and other times it was with the dramatic flair that only Reality TV can produce. No matter who was at fault, these relationships were over. Was this our new reality? Had our friendship run its course? Perhaps our bond was not strong enough to withstand the twists and turns of life.

As I pondered these questions I was heartbroken and angry. Once again I felt as if "my person," to whom I'd bared my soul and shared my fears, celebrated my triumphs and navigated the treacherous terrain of marriage and motherhood had abandoned me. How could she not "know" what I needed or "sense" that I was struggling? And what hurt most was the realization that maybe she was not heartbroken or angry—maybe she had just moved on and did not feel the loss as acutely as I had.

Just as I was 15 years earlier, I was faced with the reality that with intimacy comes vulnerability and with vulnerability there must be humility. It was time to take a good look at myself and recognize the ways in which I had pushed us to the edge. Where had I failed to "sense" and "just know?" When did I let the silence go on too long or the words be too few?

To this day I count myself lucky, because it turned out that my friend valued our friendship as much as I did. And so, we sat down together and forced our way through a long, honest (and tear-filled) conversation.

I learned since those early years that arguments and relationships do not have to end with dramatic departures, hurtful words and pointed fingers. Sometimes all that needs to happen to end a fight or salvage a relationship is an honest, hard conversation. Sometimes making yourself vulnerable one more time in order to say 'I'm sorry' or 'I was wrong' or even 'I miss you' is all it takes to bridge that gap that has grown between you and the person you love. Reminding yourself that this person was once worth the risk of authenticity and vulnerability is difficult in the heat of the moment. But if you're lucky, as I was, you can put yourself out there one final time and save that beautiful intimate relationship before it is broken forever.

*Vicky Willenberg is a wife, mother, and obsessive volunteer at her sons' school. She works in Digital Marketing and Communications while juggling the class bake sale, folding laundry from two weeks ago, and searching for the dog who escaped from the yard yet again. You can find her chronicling the good, the bad and the hilarious on her blog,* The Pursuit of Normal. *Vicky has been featured on* Scary Mommy, Mamapedia *and* Mamalode *and had the privilege of being a contributor to the* HerStories Project's *first book.*

# FRIENDSHIP IS A VERB

---

KRISTIN SHAW

Sarah and I met in 2001 at orientation for a copier company where we were both starting new jobs. We quickly discovered that our birthdays were only days apart and became fast friends. We started buying cakes for each other every year until we decided having a whole cake to ourselves wasn't really the best thing for our waistlines. We had lunch together often and hosted the office Christmas parties together. Her happy laugh and East Coast accent were fun to be around. We had scores of inside jokes and could speak to each other simply by exchanging a look.

Often, she stopped by my office to talk. Sometimes, we talked too much and I felt guilty about shooing her out so I could get some work done. She was good-natured and brought a smile to my face; even when she complained, it was funny.

Sarah saw me through my divorce and cheered me on through the Summer I Got my Groove Back. We called our movie and dinners together "date night" when we were both single, and I could count on her to be free, most of the time. We played tennis and giggled at our serves. She was the only person at my company to know when I started dating one of our colleagues from across the country, and we shared the secret conspiratorially. After he became my husband and was on the road for three weeks a month, I spent many evenings with her. When I left to move to Austin with my new husband, I was sad to leave her.

Returning to Atlanta for business was difficult, especially after I had my son. What were once trips of leisure and extended weekends turned into quick turnarounds and 30 stolen minutes of coffee on the way to another engagement. I never got to see anyone as much as I wanted; my first priority was getting home to my son.

The last time I saw Sarah, I stopped by her house to visit, with my young son in tow. She had a new dog—a fluffy Bichon Frise. For all of the years we had been friends, she had longed for a dog, but didn't have the time to support a puppy. My son and I cooed over the dog and Sarah talked about how worried she was that a coyote could sneak under the fence or an eagle would swoop down and steal her new baby.

At some point in time, she stopped returning my calls. And my texts. And my email messages. I gave her the benefit of the doubt; people are busy and messages are missed or forgotten. There was no drama; there was no blowup.

Over time, it was easy to surmise that I did or said something to hurt her feelings, but I don't know what it might have been. I sent her several messages in various ways saying: *I wish I knew why we don't speak any more.*

After months of radio silence, I gave up. It felt wrong to

give up on her, but there is a fine line between stalker and concerned former friend.

My heart feels her loss; I blame myself, because no other explanation is available. Did I spend too much time talking about my son? Did I not appreciate her puppy enough? Did I say something that offended her? Was she envious of my marriage and family? I had no idea. I was left to speculate, and the answer could just as likely have been "none of the above."

In contrast, another friend I have had for several years sent me, out of the blue, a message telling me that her feelings were hurt, and the words with which I responded always seemed to be the wrong ones. Every time I saw her name online I felt a pang of regret for what I thought could not be repaired. I didn't fully understand, but I reminded myself that her perception is her reality, and tried to see her point of view.

I took a deep breath one day, about a month or two later, and I wrote to her: *"We have been friends for too long to let this die. Let's figure it out together."* Slowly, haltingly, we exchanged messages and ideas, and started calling each other again. We're both busy working mothers of active little boys, and keeping in touch frequently is not as easy as it was years ago, but we are doing the best we can. A good friendship is always worth salvaging.

I'm a little shell-shocked, finding my way back. Once someone tells you that she thinks you're not doing a good job as a friend, or you have failed her in some way, there are many eggshells to walk upon on the road to redemption. It's hard to know when to stop bending over backward and just be yourself. You can lose yourself on the road back, wondering if you'll ever be good enough again. It has to be worth that trip back with each tiny step. I think it is, and I'm a fighter.

Although my friend's honesty was difficult to take, I much preferred the chance to stop, understand, and try to work through her feelings than the alternative. Distance and time constraints will test a friendship; it's easy to say that you don't have time for anyone who doesn't have time for you. At least with the second friend, I knew why she was upset. She gave me her reasons and I was not left to guess, and I respect her more for it.

It's the not knowing with Sarah that haunts me the most. The truth is, I miss her. Every time I hear a Keith Urban or Bon Jovi song, I think of her and the concerts we attended together. Every time a new chick flick comes out, I remember our movie dates. When I see a Carvel sign, I think of our ice cream cakes. It is all past, now.

Just recently, my son started carrying around the fuzzy, fluffy teddy bear Sarah gave me at my baby shower. I nearly gave it away once, thinking that it was a painful reminder of friendship lost. Instead, I kept it and put it on my son's bed. It's getting a little worn already; he loves that bear hard. I'm going to remind myself of the good times we had and let it go. In my mind, I have boxed up our friendship and tied a beautiful ribbon of remembrance on it.

On my wedding day, the priest reminded us that "Love is a verb; it's a choice you make every day." When it comes to marriage, it's something I remind myself of on a regular basis. What I have discovered, as I slide into middle age, is that it also applies to friendships.

Friendship is a verb. It's not a state of being, or a whim. It's something that you choose, something that you make space for in your world.

The space that was Sarah's friendship has been filled, now, pushed together by new friendships and the richness of old friendships that have become even fuller and more robust over time. If she were to come back around and ask for her space back, honestly, I'd make room. There is always more space in my heart.

*Kristin Shaw is a freelance writer, wife, and mama to a mini-Texan. In 2013, her blog* Two Cannoli *was named a* Babble *Top 100 site, and she was recognized as Type-A We Still Blog awards finalist. She's proud to be a 2013 cast member and now co-producer of the Listen To Your Mother show in Austin. She was recently named a BlogHer Voice of the Year reader for 2014, and she writes for the* Huffington Post. *Born in Hackensack, NJ, and raised in Elkhart, Indiana, she has steadily moved south through Ohio, Georgia, and down to Texas, and she rarely misses snow.*

# SUNSHINE AND STORM

---

KATRINA WILLS

There is still a scar, a reminder of both the joy and pain her friendship brought me. But I no longer examine it to see if it's pink or if it's fading. I leave it alone. I must.

From the beginning, people told us we would either love or hate each other—that that there'd be no in-between. And, in retrospect, that's where our 20-year friendship existed.

Sunshine and storm. Fire and ice.

Jackie (that's what we'll call her) was the best friend I could ever wish for... when she chose to be. She was feisty, fun, affectionate, supportive, thoughtful. But like every other human being, there was another side to her as well: volatile, dismissive, fickle, angry, accusatory.

For years, our families were intertwined. We walked in and out of each other's homes like they were our own. Her kids called me "Aunt." She was there for the births of all my four children. We loved each other fiercely, laughed without inhibition.

Until we no longer did.

We vacationed together, basking in the sun, cooking in rented kitchens. We sat together on basketball sidelines, cheering for our collective kids. She raided my closet and threw out all my frumpy "Mom" clothes. She convinced me to grow my hair longer, taught me how to walk in heels. We drank vodka and wine, we threw parties and sat poolside. I held her kids, and she held mine.

We discussed books and movies and parenting and politics and life. Our visions were never aligned, but they were complementary. We respected each other's differences, entertained alternative points of view.

She's beautiful, Jackie. I used to call her My Jackie. I was proud to be her friend, content to walk through life side by side.

Of course, it wasn't always goodness and light. No relationships are. From early on, my husband Chris and I always joked about Jackie's "Friend du Jour." A new girl would enter her life—a colleague, a neighbor, a fellow churchgoer—and Jackie would move out of mine. I'd watch from the sidelines, time and time again, as she and another female friend would spend all their waking hours together, would share the space we once inhabited.

She liked to separate her friendships into pretty little boxes, anxious about different facets of her life mingling with one another. For months after she'd moved into her new neighborhood, Chris and I were not invited to gatherings.

"It feels weird," she explained. "I don't know if I'm ready for my neighborhood friends to meet my college friends."

I didn't understand that separation, that sentiment. I was always eager to introduce Jackie to my other friends, my neighbors, my extended family. I was proud of her.

I wanted to be with her. I loved everything about her—including her volatility.

"Why do you let her do that to you?" mutual friends asked. "Doesn't it hurt?" And it did. It hurt a great deal. I loved that Jackie had a wide berth of friends—I did, too—but when she latched on to another woman, Jackie squeezed me out of her life. She could not figure out how to make that situation an "and" instead of an "or." And it happened over and over and over again. We'd talk about it, argue about it, retreat to our corners licking our wounds. We'd spend time apart, trying to figure out whether to move forward. Ultimately, I would go to her—I hated conflict, was always the peacemaker—and break the silence. I was the fence-mender. I loved her, and I wanted her in my life, and I knew that apologies were not part of her repertoire.

Before our final break-up, our relationship went downhill fast. She was quick to anger, flinging accusations and biting words around like knives. "You never take responsibility for anything!" she shouted at me after I'd failed to put enough sunscreen on her daughter during a summer outing. She screamed at me in front of my kids. I was shocked, stunned, angry.

She hurt me many times during our 20 years together. I'm certain I hurt her, too. Friendships—along with their successes and their failures—are never one-sided. They are intricate webs of experiences and actions and interpretations. Blame and finger-pointing go both ways. I'm sure she has a laundry list of grievances against me. I'm not always easy. I can be needy and moody and selfish and insensitive. I hold grudges and burn bridges. I'm certain there were times when I let her down.

When our friendship finally came to an end, it was a

bitter conclusion. I was in the midst of publishing my first book, training for my first marathon, planning a move 500 miles away. I wanted her to be a part of everything, to be mired in the ups and downs with me, but she chose differently.

I was not what she needed.

After years of painful reflection and contemplation, I still don't know what exactly went wrong. And after all this time, I guess it doesn't really matter. What I do know is this: she stopped talking to me, and I never went back to find out why. As time continued to tick away, our friendship faded, leaving a sad emptiness in its wake.

For many days and nights, I cried. I thought about all the things that might have gone wrong; I lamented all that we had missed. She didn't attend my first book signing, my marathon, our going away party. Five hundred miles away from her, the ache of loneliness wrapped itself around my heart... and Jackie was at the core of it.

I missed her. I hated her. I loved her. I blamed her. Eventually, I forgave her.

The end of our friendship wasn't just about us. It was about our families as well. My kids missed her kids. They didn't understand what went wrong. I didn't know how to explain it to them. Our husbands stopped talking, our mutual friends took sides, even though we didn't ask them to. It's a natural course of action, I suppose, the choosing. Ending a relationship is awkward and painful and uncomfortable. There are multiple sides to every story, and not all are visible or heard.

The end of a relationship in the age of social media exacerbates the hurt in many ways. I watched as she posted pictures of her friends—her new friends, our former friends—attending dinners, concerts, parties. She looked happy, content. I sat alone in my new, unfamiliar home and cried. I was homesick and heartsick.

It took years to get through the stages of grief. Anger was the hardest. I was furious with her for caring so little, for giving up so easily, for shutting us out of her life so completely. One moment, I wanted to drive the ten hours to her house and demand an explanation. And the next, I wanted to call and cry and tell her how much I missed her. I rode a roller coaster of emotions. There was no easy way through the pain. Love and hate are such close kin, driven by passion and fueled with fire. It's indifference that hurts. And that's where she left me.

One day, I sat down with a box filled with cards and letters from our past. Like I would have done with the remnants from a former lover, I surrounded myself with her words—with her promises of forever friendship, her witty quips, her expressions of gratitude. *Liar*, I thought. *Bitch. Your actions speak so loudly, I can't hear what you're saying*. And then I cried. For a long, lonely time, I cried. When I was done, I packed up all the cards and letters and took a deep breath.

Today I hold the memory of our friendship in a small, protected pocket of my heart. It resides there, a reminder of all that was good and right. I've let go of what was bad, what was wrong, what tore us to pieces. There were no answers, no explanations. There never will be. There is just today, tomorrow, and all that remains.

My life is good and full, and I am happy. I have an adoring husband, fabulous kids, a circle of faithful, funny, and cherished friends. I learned from Jackie. She taught me many things. Perhaps the most important lesson I learned from her is this: I am alive and filled with joy and worthy of love and acceptance. Life is too short to lament *what might have been.* There is far too much of *what comes next.*

Anger and disappointment and grief will eat you alive if you let them. When loss comes—as it so often does—a journey through grief is inevitable.

But it's no place to reside.

I choose the other side, where love and forgiveness abound. And most importantly, even when someone else might not, I choose me.

*Katrina Anne Willis, a Hoosier currently living in Ohio, is happily married to her high school sweetheart and is the mother of four teens/tweens. An author and essayist, Katrina was named a 2011 Midwest Writers Fellow, was a 2011 "Notes & Words" contest finalist, participated in the 2013 Indianapolis "Listen to Your Mother" show, is a writer for* Mamalode *and is resident "Mom" blogger for* Indy's Child *magazine. She's the author of* Table for Six: The Extraordinary Tales of an Ordinary Family, *is featured in A Band of Women's 2014 "Nothing but the Truth" anthology, and was awarded the 2014 Parenting Media Association's Gold Medal Blogger Award.*

# ACKNOWLEDGMENTS

---

We are grateful to so many who provided us with guidance, wisdom, and advice.

First, we are eternally indebted to Lauren Apfel, a brilliant writer in her own right. She was truly much more than an editor on this project; she was an advisor, editing mentor, and good friend.

We are grateful to our wonderful friends in the blogging and writing community: Deb Cole, Kristi Campbell, Nina Badzin, Sarah Rudell Beach, Rachel Demas, Katia Bishofs, Jen Kehl, Kim Morand, Sarah Shaw Almond.

We'd like to thank the hundreds of women who opened their hearts and memory banks to us for our survey and with their own stories. Your openness and bravery touched us.

# ABOUT THE EDITORS

**Jessica Smock** is a writer, educator, former teacher, researcher, and mom to a toddler son. She lives in Buffalo, New York with her family, their Boston terrier, and very bossy cat. She earned her doctorate in educational policy and development from Boston University last year and is a Phi Beta Kappa graduate of Wesleyan University. She writes about parenting, education, and books at her blog, School of Smock. Her writing and expertise have been featured on the Huffington Post, the Brain Child website, Scary Mommy, iVillage, the *Chicago Tribune*, and Babble.

**Stephanie Sprenger** is a freelance writer, music therapist, and mother of two young daughters. She writes about parenthood and women's issues at stephaniesprenger.com, and her work has been featured on various websites, including the Huffington Post, Mamalode, In the Powder Room, BlogHer, and Scary Mommy. Stephanie performed in the Denver production of Listen To Your Mother in May 2013, and she was honored to be named one of BlogHer's 2014 Voices of the Year. She lives in Colorado with her family, and can usually be found behind a guitar, in front of her laptop, or underneath a pile of laundry.

# FOR MORE INFORMATION

**Welcome to the HerStories Project Community!**
To find out more information and to read more about our contributors, our latest call for submissions, and our writing classes, please visit:
**http://www.herstoriesproject.com**
Be sure to subscribe to our newsletter to stay up to date with The HerStories Project! You can also find us on Twitter: @herstoriestales and on Facebook. You can also reach us at info@herstoriesproject.com. We'd love to hear your comments and stories!

Made in the USA
San Bernardino, CA
09 March 2017